MW01531966

Perry Family
in
Maine

Its
Ancestors
and
Descendants

By
Rev. Charles Nelson Sinnett
Carthage, South Dakota

A HERITAGE CLASSIC

Lewiston, ME
1911

Blemishes, foxing, and discoloration are characteristics of older books, and
may show through to some extent, in reprints such as this. We feel the
content of this book warrants its reissue despite these blemishes.
We hope you agree, and read on with pleasure.

A Facsimile Reprint
Published 2003 by

HERITAGE BOOKS, INC.
1540-E Pointer Ridge Place
Bowie, Maryland 20716
1-800-398-7709

WWW.HERITAGEBOOKS.COM

ISBN: 0-7884-2313-4

A Complete Catalog Listing Hundreds of Titles
On History, Genealogy, and Americana
Available Free Upon Request.

OUR PERRY FAMILY IN MAINE

Its Ancestors and Descendants

By REV. CHARLES NELSON SINNETT

Carthage, Miner County, South Dakota

(1) JOHN PERRY. He was the son of John Perry of Foreham, Hampshire County, England, and died 1621; m. Judith ———. John Perry was born in London, England, Nov., 1604; died at Watertown, Mass., 1674, "aged 61 years." He was apprenticed Nov. 26, 1621, fr seven years, to John Lawson, a Clothier of London, and was a widely-known workman at that trade. He came to Watertown, Mass., about 1666. He m. Johanna Holland, who died in 1667. She was the daughter of Joseph Holland, a clothworker of London, England. The names of their following three children have been found.

(2) JOHN PERRY. (2) ELIZABETH PERRY. (2) JOSIAH PERRY.

* * *

(2) JOHN PERRY b. in England, 1644; d. at Watertown, Mass., before Dec., 1724; he is mentioned in his grandfather's will; m. Dec. 13, 1667, Sarah Clary b. Oct. 4, 1647, d. at Cambridge, Mass., Oct. 11, 1730; the daughter of John Clary of Watertown, Mass., and of Mary Cassell. The following records of their children were found in the history of North Brookfield, Mass.

(3) JOHN PERRY b. Oct. 1, 1668; d. Nov. 8, 1668.

(3) JOHN PERRY b. Mch. 3, 1669-70; resided in Cambridge, Mass., where he died previous to 1730; m. July 19, 1693, Sarah Price, b. Sept. 27, 1667; the daughter of William Price and Mary Marblehead of Watertown, Mass.

(3) Johannah Perry b. Nov. 6, 1672.

(3) Sarah Perry b. July 11, 1675; d. in youth.

(3) Joseph Perry b. Dec. 7, 1677; d. Nov., 1680.

(3) Elizabeth Perry b. Oct. 2, 1781.

(3) Josiah Perry b. Nov. 28, 1684; d. in Worcester, Mass., Sept. 16, 1767. See Fuller records on following page.

(3) Joseph Perry b. Jan. 17, 1690-91.

(3) Sarah Perry b. 1694.

THE RECORDS OF JOSIAH PERRY (3).

(3) JOSIAH PERRY, the eighth child of John Perry (2) and Sarah Clary, was b. in Watertown, Mass., Nov. 28, 1684, and d. at Worcester, Mass., Sept. 16, 1767. He was a man of the same sturdy, religious character which characterized his ancestors and a long line of descendants. He m. (1st) Jan. 12, 1708, Berthiah Cutter b. Cambridge, Mass., Dec. 2, 1686; baptized in Watertown, Mass., Aug. 18, 1689; d. Oct. 1735; she was the daughter of Ephraim Cutter and Berthia Wood. Her line of descent was; (1) Samuel Cutter, who d. in England, his widow, Elizabeth Cutter, quite advanced in years, coming to America in 1640. The supposition is that several married daughters of hers came to America about the time of her emigration. One of these (2), Isabella Cutter, was the wife of Thomas Sweetman of Cambridge, Mass. Their daughter, (3) Elizabeth Sweetman, b. Jan. 6, 1646-7, m. Dec. 7, 1671, Benjamin Wellington, and their daughter (4) Mehitabel Wellington, b. Mch. 4, 1687-8; died Sept. 13, 1775; m. William Sherman; and their son (5) Roger Sherman, the Signer of the Declaration of Independence, was b. April 19, 1721. Richard Cutter (2), the younger son of Widow Elizabeth Cutter, was very likely a voyager to America on the ship with his mother. He was a cooper by trade, and was admitted as a Freeman in 1641. This privilege was earnestly desired by every man, and all freemen of that period were required to be orthodox members of the Church, twenty years old, and worth two hundred pounds. In 1643 he became a member of the Artillery Company. About 1644 he married Elizabeth, whose surname is unknown. Her tombstone is one of the oldest now standing in the ancient burying-ground of Old Cambridge, Mass.: "Here lyes ye body of Elizabeth Cutter, wife to Richard Cutter, aged about 42 years; died March 5, 1661-2." Richard Cutter married (2d), Feb. 14, 1662-3, Mrs. Frances (Perriman) Amsden of Cambridge, the widow of Richard Amsden; she survived Richard's decease. Richard Cutter's residence was in Menotomy. He requested to be buried in "Cambridge Buryingplace near his first wife's grave." His monumental stones are in the western part of the yard, and the inscription is perfectly legible: "Here lyes ye body of Richard Cutter, aged about 72 years, died ye 16 of June, 1693." In his will he mentions daughters, and the five sons, Samuel, William,

Ephraim, Gershom and Nathaniel of the (3d) generation. Of these (3) Ephraim Cutter appears first at Watertown, Mass., Aug. 18, 1689, where three of his children were baptized. Ephraim Cutter is mentioned in the will of his father, and that of his brother William. The date of his decease is unknown; he was b. 1651; he was a soldier and probably captain in King Philip's War. He m. Berthiah Wood, the daughter of Nicholas Wood and Marcy Williams of Medfield, Mass., b. July 28, 1659-60, and d. Sept. 18, 1731. His children were: (4) Ephraim, (4) Jonathan, (4) Berthiah Cutter b. Cambridge, Mass., Dec. 2, 1686, and married Josiah Perry, as noted above.

JOSIAH PERRY m. (2d) March 10, 1736, Elizabeth Harrington who d. Sept. 26, 1748 (62). The following children were all of the marriage of Josiah Perry with Berthiah Cutter, and were all born in Watertown, Mass.:

(4) Jonathan Perry b. Jan. 1, 1710.
(4) Lydia Perry b. Dec. 8, 1711.
(4) Josiah Perry b. Feb. 8, 1714.
(4) Ephraim Perry b. Nov. 11, 1715.
(4) Nathan Perry b. May 20, 1718.
(4) Berthia Perry b. Jan. 31, 1719.
(4) Mary Perry b. Feb. 13, 1721.
(4) Isaiah Perry b. Feb. 8, 1723.
(4) Dorcas Perry b. Dec., 1727.
(4) Sarah Perry b. 1728.

Our line of Perry history continues with the fourth child in this list; (4) Ephraim Perry b. Nov. 11, 1715. He m. (1st) in 1742 Hannah Holbrook, b. Sept. 11, 1720; d. June 27, 1744; m. (2d) Mrs. Mary Deland Badcock b. Feb. 28, 1725, d. "1745." Her family line was: (1) Robert Badcock, who was a Rater for Dorchester, Mass., in 1657; Supervisor of the Highways, 1660; Selectman of Milton, Mass., 1678-1691, and probably for other years, and was also Captain. In 1672 he bought land "beyond Medfield at that place commonly called Bogistow," now Sherborn, and at Natick; he d. Nov. 12, 1694; and his widow, Joanna, d. Dec. 4, 1700 (71). His son, (2) Ebenezer Badcock, was b. at Milton, Mass., Oct. 2, 1762; lived in Sherborn, Mass., where he d. Dec. 15, 1717; m. Hannah Barbour of Medfield, Mass. Their son (3) Ebenezer Badcock b. Sept. 4, 1697, d. Mch. 27, 1730; m. May 3, 1704, Abigail Leland, daughter of Hopstill Leland and Mary Ballard of Sherborn, Mass. Their daughter

(4) Mary married Ephraim Perry. The children of Ephraim Perry were all of this second marriage with Mrs. Mary (Deland) Badcock, the first four children being born at Sherborn, Mass.

(5) EBENEZER PERRY b. Mch. 27, 1746, was alive in Boston, Mass., in 1780.

(5) JESSE PERRY b. Oct. 22, 1747; resided in Westminster, Vt., and probably married Achsah Fairbanks.

(5) CAPTAIN JOHN PERRY b. Oct. 30, 1749; d. North Haven, Me., Jan. 14, 1833 (84); see full records page 8.

(5) JONATHAN PERRY b. Dec. 7, 1751, probably d. Dec. 18, 1751.

(5) MARY PERRY b. about 1753; probably died 1843 (90); m. Samuel Eaton. General Adelbert Ames, "I remember her well."

(6) SARAH EATON m. William Gary of Thomaston, Me. (6) Eliza Eaton married James Rivers, or Reeves. (6) Melicent Eaton m. Robert Perry; see records. Chapter eight. (6) May d. Boston.

(5) WILDER PERRY b. about 1755; d. in Boston, 1780. In 1779 he was a Revolutionary soldier at the Fox Islands, Me.; and a sailor in the State service. Probably unmarried. From the Mass. Archives, Vol. 232, page 219 A and 219 B, Aug. 26, 1780. Mr. Ebenezer Perry to Philip Eckert, Dr., to making your brother's coffin 75 pounds. Received payment.

Philip Eckert.

1780. State of Massachusetts Bay to Ephm. Perry, Dr. To twelve days attendance on Wilder Perry at 20 pounds, 240 pounds. In the service and pay of this State a Maren (marine) on board the ship Protector, John Foster Williams, Commander.

To a Grave and Attendance, 130 pounds.

To a Coffin, 150 pounds. Total 520 pounds.

Ephraim Perry.

Mass. Archives: Vol. 232, page 220;

To the Honorable Senate & House of Representatives:

The petition of Ephraim Perry truly sheweth that his son Wilder Perry was aboard the State Ship Protector on her last cruize, and was taken sick with the distemper that prevailed on board said ship, and died some time after his return to Boston. Your petitioner was at great expense for burying and funeral charges, which he conceives ought to be paid by the Government, especially as your petitioner has been drove off his estate and deprived of his interest by the enemy at Penobscot, and obliged to take refuge from their malice in this part of the Government. He therefore humbly requests your honors to give orders for the payment of the annexed account, which will in some measure relieve his present distress, and as in duty bound shall ever pray.

Ephraim Perry.

Medfield, Jan. 6, 1781.

Mass. Archives, page 219.

Commonwealth of Massachusetts in the House of Representatives Feb., 1781.

On petition of Ephraim Perry saying that he ought to be paid for the expense of nursing, funeral charges, etc., of his son, Wilder Perry, a sailor on board the Ship Protector in her last cruize, who died in a private house in this town, and received no supply from the State Hospital—

Therefore *Resolved,* That the said Ephraim Perry be paid out of the Treasury of this Commonwealth the sum of Ninety-six Pounds in full for his Expense of Rations, Nursing, etc., Funeral Charges, of said Wilder Perry.

Sent in for Concurrence,

CALEB DAVIS, *Speaker.*

In Senate, April 19, 1781; Read and Concurred. Jere Powell, President.

Approved, JOHN HANCOCK.

(5) EPHRAIM CUTLER PERRY b about 1757; baptized Holden, Mass., June 27, 1756. He was a brave soldier and was severely wounded in the Revolutionary War. M. Nov. 7, 1782, Anna Plimpton, Rev. Samuel Stillman performing the ceremony.

(5) HANNAH PERRY b. about 1760-1762; d. about 1852; m. June 25, 1789 by Rev. Samuel Stillman, Captain Judah Bacon of Boston, Mass. "He was a very wealthy man, but lost his property, and his wife became very poor, and was aided by the Free Masons, and also by her brother, John Perry of North Haven, Me. She went from North Haven, Me., to live with her grandson, George Redding, who had a book store on Milk St., or near there, Boston; he is said to have been connected with the Boston Mercantile Journal. The mother of Gen. Adelbert Ames visited some of these Reddings in 1843, but the name of the family is not mentioned in the Boston City Directory; but there are quite a number of people of that name in N. Y. City; but in corres-

pondence with them I did not find any connection between them
and our Perry Line. Redding's Salve, which was once such a
popular remedy, was made by some of the family in Boston.
Captain Bacon was called 'Jeddah' in some of the old records.
He was buried by the Free Masons and some Mercantile Company. He is said to have come from 'Cape Cod way.'"

THE RECORDS OF CAPTAIN JOHN PERRY (5)

(5) CAPTAIN JOHN PERRY, according to the family records,
was b. Sherborn, Mass., Oct. 30, 1749, and d. North Haven, Me.,
Jan. 14, 1833 (84). An old family tradition stated that he was
born at Duxbury, Mass., in 1741. One such account gave the
date of his birth as Nov. 10, 1750 and stated that he was 90
years old at the time of his death. But we can safely accept the
Town records, and also the clear statement of Gen. Adelbert
Ames of Lowell, Mass., who has given much time and study to
this matter. "I have looked all over the Duxbury, Mass., records
and failed to find there any mention of the birth of John Perry.
But the Sherborn, Mass., records give us the right date. He died
in 1833 and was eighty-four years old. I have lately visited his
grave at North Haven, Me., with my Uncle Hezekiah Ames, who
was thirteen years old at the time of John Perry's death, and he
attended his funeral. At the time of his death John Perry was a
member of the family of the father of this Hezekiah Ames, and
was buried from his house. My father, John Ames, who was
twenty-five years old when John Perry died, told me that he was
always known as 'Boston Perry,' and that he had often gone
gunning where the Quincy Market in Boston now stands."
    From Wilder Washington Perry, "During the winter of 1780,
which was a very cold one, John Perry made a trip in his sloop
of some ten or twelve tons to Connecticut to visit his brother,
and while there he was frozen in a river so that he could not get
back as soon as he expected to. He wrote home to his wife, 'Pull
the hay from the mow with a hook (to make it last longer), and
give my love to the brothers and sisters in the Church.' He was
evidently afraid that the boys would waste the hay while he was
gone." Gen. Adelbert Ames says, "This brother whom he

visited must have been Jonathan or Jesse, for his brother Wilder died that year, and Ebenezer was with him in Boston."

The following sketch of Captain John Perry is taken from a short history of Vinalhaven, Me., written by O. P. Lyons, 1889, and read at the Centennial celebration of that town: "John Perry came to the Fox Islands about 1764. He settled on what is now known as Crabtree's Point, a part of North Haven. He also took up a lot of land between Perry's Creek and Seal Cove, on the south Island, Vinalhaven. About 1779 he was living on this south Island, where he cultivated a small patch of land. He was one of those who suffered much from foraging parties during the occupancy of Castine, Me., by the British. The family traditions assert that he was stoutly hated by the English because, when his neighbors all wished to take a neutral position during the Revolutionary War, he firmly refused to do so, though he should lose all that he had. One day a party of fifteen foragers landed at his place and were helping themselves to his crops, evidently thinking that one man would not dare to resist them. But Perry, selecting a favorable spot, shot two of the party and then fled into the woods. The remainder of the foragers pursued him, but he evaded them by hiding in the trunk of a hollow tree. He remained in this hiding place about forty-eight hours, when it appeared that the coast was clear, and he hurried to the shore, sprang into his dug-out, and paddled to Owl's Head. From thence he went to Boston, but he shortly afterwards returned to his Island farm, and, when this became known to the British, strenuous efforts were made to capture him, but without success. Several times he came near falling into the hands of the enemy, but he always managed to escape. Once, while picking up some sea fowl which he had shot, in the vicinity of Crockett's River, some British appeared on the scene and ordered him to come ashore. He answered that he would land as soon as he had picked up the ducks. His would-be-captors stood carelessly watching him as they thought that he was completely in their power. It was this fact, no doubt, which he keenly observed, for, while pretending to be getting ready to go ashore, he suddenly, with all his might, paddled in the opposite direction. A shower of bullets followed him, but he escaped unharmed. He is said to have been a man of small stature, but full of the pluck and endurance which have characterized so many of his well-known descendants." An account from a Rockland, Maine, journal states, "After Captain John Perry had killed the two men who were stealing his corn, the enemy burned his house and destroyed or carried off everything on the premises, and, when the matter was reported to the British headquarters, a proclamation was issued offering a reward for Perry's capture, dead or alive. He came to the mainland, and erected a house at what is now Rockland Highlands, on the spot where the residence of Hon. S. M. Bird stands to-day. A party of British and Tories was made up to effect his capture, but he obtained information that they were coming, and he was not at home. They burned his new house and destroyed everything about it. Captain Perry then thought it time to devote his sole attention to fighting the invaders, and, procuring a small vessel, and enlisting a crew, he obtained a commission as Captain and did excellent service during the remainder of the Revolutionary War. The British were soon glad to leave that part of the Maine coast."

The copy of the following petition was taken from the Massachusets Archives, Vol. 171, page 465. It was forwarded to Governor John Hancock of Massachusetts, 1781.

COMMONWEALTH OF MASS:

>   *To His Excellency the Governor and the Honorable*
Council:

The subscribers, Inhabitants of the town of St. George, in the County of Lincoln, humbly represent to your Excellency and Honors, the Distressing Situation of the Inhabitants of that part of the Commonwealth who are friends to the liberties and Independence of the United States. Being nigh the Enemy, and having no men to Guard, they are continually exposed, and frequently Experience the ravages of the Enemy, the insults and Abuse of the more Infernal Tories, who still reside Amongst us, who now pretend the Government has given us up and will take no further Measure for our Defense, which greatly disheartens many of the friends of the Country. We would likewise inform your Excellency & Honors that there is now Allmost a Free and Uninterrupted Trade carried on between the Enemy and the Inhabitants near Penobscot which we Fear unless speedily checked will prove greatly prejudicial to the Commonwealth. We therefore most humbly & Earnestly pray that such a number of men as you judge necessary may be stationed near Bagaduce to stop the ravages of the Enemy & curb the Insolence of the Cursed Tories, and also pray that you will please to grant a Commission in the name of John Perry for the Boat Fly, which is not intended for the purpose of plundering, (which your petitioners abhor and detest) but for the sole purpose of Interrupting the Trade between the Inhabitants & the Enemy; and your petitioners as in Duty bound shall ever pray.

In behalf of the Inhabitants of St. George.

JOHN PERRY,

THOMAS THOMPSON.

The granting of this Commission to Captain John Perry is dated Aug. 21, 1781, and is as follows:

Council: Advised that John Perry be Commissioned as Commander of said Boat Fly for the purpose above mentioned, he complying with the resolves of Congress.

JOHN W. AVERY, *Secretary.*

Mass. Archives, Vol. 171, page 487.

To His Excellency, the Governor, and the Hon'ble Council of the Commonwealth of Mass'tts.

The petition of Ebenezer May and others of Boston, Humbly sheweth;

That your petitioners have fitted out a small boat of about three tons burthen, to be navigated by ten men and well armed with Musquets, and intended to cruise near the enemy's Lines at Penobscot, & prevent if possible any communication with the Enemy. Said vessel to join Company with a Boat commanded by Captain John Perry, to whom your Excellencyes & Honors granted a Comission yesterday.

I certify the foregoing to be true extracts from the Mass. Archives in the custody of this office. Witness the Seal of the Commonwealth. Isaac H. Edgett, Deputy Secretary.

In 1785 three settlers of Fox Islands, Me., petitioned the General Court that they be granted full possession of the several islands then known as the Fox Islands, and among the names of the petitioners appear the names of John Perry, Ephraim Perry and William Perry. One writes, "I have never considered that these two last petitioners were relatives of John Perry, though we know that he had a brother Ephraim."

Several relics of Captain John Perry have been mentioned by various correspondents, but so far it has been impossible to secure good descriptions or pictures of these. Mr. Jarvis C. Perry, Rockland, Maine, writes, "The old flint-lock gun with which John Perry took summary vengeance on his Majesty's soldiers while robbing his cornfield is still in the possession of a family at Appleton, Me. I tried to buy it awhile since, but without success."

Mrs. William Perry, Vinalhaven, Me., "I know nothing about the gun with which Ancestor John Perry killed the Englishmen. But Mrs. Roxana Dyer has the kettle in which John Perry made a stew on the day when he shot his enemies, and I have often seen it at her house."

Captain John Perry married (1st) Feb. 19, 1808, Lucy Wooster b. May 9, 1759; d. Dec., 1832; m. (2d) Mrs. Perry, who was probably the widow of William Perry (though these two families were not relatives), whose three children by a former marriage have often been counted as the children of Capt. John Perry. There were no children of this second marriage.

Lucy Wooster, the first wife, was a woman of great executive ability. She was the daughter of David Wooster and Lucy Crockett. David Wooster is said to have been born in Chester, or Cheshire, England, Feb. 22, 1732, and d. Aug. 28, 1808 (74) ; after the death of his parents he came to America with an Uncle when he was but twelve years old, 1744. He is said to have first landed at Boston, Mass. He learned a spar maker's trade and worked at it in Falmouth, now Portland, Maine. In 1760 he bought a beautiful piece of timber land at what is now North Haven, Me., and began clearing it off. Another account says that David Wooster was spar maker to the King of England, and came to Portland, Me., to mark trees that were suitable for spars. After his marriage he settled at North Haven at what is known as the Edward Wooster Place, and on this Captain John Perry is buried. His wife is said to have been of Falmouth, Me., and was probably the daughter of Thomas Crockett who was at Kittery, Me., in 1633. She was classed among the best physicians of her time on account of her great skill in caring for and curing people who were afflicted with various diseases. It is said that David Wooster and his wife had six children: David, Joseph, Nathaniel, Lucy, Lydia, who married John Smith of Smithfield, R. I.; and Margaret who married William Vinal of Boston,

Mass., after whom Vinalhaven, Me., was named. All these children settled at North Haven, Me.

The children of Captain John Perry and Lucy Wooster.

(6) JOHN PERRY, Jr., b. July 19, 1776; d. uly 10, 1849; he was a mariner, and resided at North Haven, Me.; m. Rachel Walton of the Fox Islands, Me.; no children.

(6) BETSEY PERRY b. Sept. 28, 1777; m. June 21, 1800, Isaac Collamore of Bristol, Me.

(7) RACHEL COLLAMORE; m. Mr. Abbott for her 2d husband.

(7) REBECCA COLLAMORE; m. Mr. Moody.

(7) PEGGY COLLAMORE; married.

(7) POLLY COLLAMORE; m. Mr. Raymond.

(7) LUCY COLLAMORE; m. Mr. Larry.

(7) PETER COLLAMORE b. about 1807; d. Sept. 30, 1891 (91—4—20); m. Rizpah Richards, and lived in Rockland, Me.

(8) "They had fourteen children: Thomas Collamore b. 1839; Priscilla b. 1846; Mary b. 1848; Ann, m. Mr. Packard, no children; Hannah J. m. Mr. Johnson, one child, a daughter.

(8) BENJAMIN E. COLLAMORE (called by some the 2d child) b. about 1825; lime burner at Rockland, Me.; m. 1852, Elizabeth Murphy. Children: (9) Hannah J. Collamore b. 1853, m. Mr. Johnson and has (10) one daughter; (9) Benjamin F. b. 1855, m. Miss Snow; children (10) Ada A.; Elma, deceased; Maud B. (9) Leonard F. Collamore b. 1858, m. Miss Weymouth and has (10) five children. (9) Patience Collamore b. 1860; (9) Elizabeth, m. Mr. Marshall and has (10) three children; (9) Robert H., m. Miss Doyley, no children; (9) Fred S., m. Miss Wheeler; (9) Addison P. Collamore, m. Miss Johnson, child (10) dead.

(7) JOHN COLLAMORE b. about 1832, lived Rockland, Me., m. 1853, Margaret Richardson; (8) Margaret E. Collamore b. 1857; (8) Emma A. Collamore b. 1858.

(6) CAPTAIN DAVID PERRY b. Aug. 7, 1779; d. Bailey's Island, Harpswell, Me., Sept. 19, 1818; m. Jane Alexander. See full records of children and descendants in Chapter One.

(6) WILDER PERRY b. Mch. 29, 1781; d. Mch. 11, 1850; m. Hannah Young. Full records of children and descendants, Chapter Two.

(6) HANNAH PERRY b. Feb. 18, 1784; d. Oct. 11, 1867; m. John Ames. Full records of children, etc., Chapter Three.

(6) LUCY PERRY b. April 13, 1785; d. Feb. 23, 1851; m. Benjamin Thomas of Rockland, Me. Full records Chapter Four.

(6) CAPT. EPHRAIM PERRY b. Dec. 21, 1788; d. Rockland, Me., May 10, 1862; m. Lucy Crockett. Full records Chapter Five.

(6) MARY PERRY b. June 27, 1790; d. Oct. 7, 1867; m. Ezekiel Raymond. Full records Chapter Six.

(6) MARGARET PERRY b. Feb. 2, 1792; d. June 20, 1859; m. David Philbrooks. Full records Chapter Seven.

(6) CAPT. ROBERT PERRY b. April 21, 1794; d. of yellow fever in N. Y. City, June 31, 1851; m. Dolly Spear and Milicent Eaton. Full records Chapter Eight.

(6) ELONIA PERRY b. Feb. 7, 1796; d. Jan. 27, 1857 (61); m. Nov. 16, 1817, Moses Hurd (Heard). Full records Chapter Nine.

(6) JAMES PERRY b. Dec. 17, 1797; died on shipboard from Southern Fever, Sept. 18, 1818; a noble man; buried beside his brother Captain David Perry at Harpswell Center, Me.; unm.

(6) REBECCA PERRY b. June 22, 1801; d. Aug. 22, 1870; m. Daniel Thomas and Samuel Moody. Full records Chapter Ten.

CHAPTER ONE

THE RECORDS OF CAPTAIN DAVID PERRY (6)

* * *

(6) CAPTAIN DAVID PERRY, the third child of Captain John Perry and Lucy Wooster, b. Vinalhaven, Me., Aug. 7, 1779; d. at Bailey's Island, Harpswell, Me., Sept. 19, 1818. He was a man of truly noble spirit and greatly beloved by the many who knew him. Early in life he became Captain of a coasting vessel plying between Vinalhaven and Rockland, Me., and Boston, Mass. One of his account books, which is now owned by Rev. C. N. Sinnett, shows well the straightforward and careful manner in which all his business affairs were conducted. After his marriage in 1804 he removed to Bailey's Island, Harpswell, Me., where he bought a cozy home, and from this Island he made many successful voyages to Southern ports. On his last trip thither for a load of hard pine his brother James, and several of the sailors, were stricken down with Southern Fever. During his faithful care of his brother Captain Perry was seized with the same disease, and lived but a short time after reaching Portland, Me. On one of his early trips from Rockland to Portland, Me., Captain David Perry was overtaken by a fierce storm. While some of the crew were complaining that there would be no safe harbor for them, Captain Perry said cheerily, "We shall find a safe shelter at Mackerel Cove, on Bailey's Island. I know lots of Harpswell people, and they have the true kind of hospitality." It was while thus outriding the storm in Mackerel Cove that he met the noble woman, Jane Alexander, who became his wife. He admired her sturdy way of working, and she admired, among many other traits of his, his efforts to keep his crew in good spirits. While doing this cheery work he went to Jaquish Island, just south of Bailey's Island, to shoot some ducks. While hastily loading his flint-lock gun, it was discharged while he was putting the powder into the pan, and the ram-rod was shot through his hand, one finger being so shattered that it was removed by Major Rowe, who then kept a store at the lower end of Bailey's Island. He bore the pain of this accident in the most

heroic manner. During the 1812 War the English lay off the
Maine coast waiting for a favorable chance to sail up the Kenne-
bec River and capture Bath. Captain David Johnson raised a
Company of men on Bailey's Island and marched them quickly
away for the defense of Bath, Me. Two men whose hands were
disabled were left on the Island to protect it from foragers, one
being Richard Orr and the other Captain David Perry. The
crew of an English crusier was watching these movements and
thought the Island unprotected, so they stood in shore, and sent
a large boat to seize all the sheep they could. As they drew near
the shore Captain Perry from behind a cliff ordered them to halt,
and, when the order was unheeded, a ringing volley rattled about
the boat. The men quickly backed water, thinking that a large
number of Yankees were lying in ambush for them. They
caught sight of a number of men's hats among the rocks and
spruce trees, and more bullets rained upon them. They hastily
retreated to their ship, and that vessel moved eastward, thinking
that Bath, Me., was not so well protected as they imagined.
Captain Perry laughed heartily when he saw that he and three
other men, with a number of women, among them his wife, had
scared off a whole boat-load of Englishmen. Some of these
women had donned the old clothing of their hubands, and made a
good Regiment. "You have done so well, that you do not need
me any longer," laughed Captain David Perry. So he kissed
his wife, jumped into a boat, rowed away to the New Meadows
River, and from thence walked to Bath, and joined his comrades.
The old flint-lock gun which he carried that day has been preserved among his descendants. Captain David Perry m. June
29, 1804, Jane Alexander, b. Harpswell, Me., April 15, 1784; d.
Bailey's Island, Harpswell, Me., June 5, 1861. She was a
daughter of Samuel Alexander and Rosannah Clark, and
through her Alexander Line was descended from the Alexanders.
who settled at Topsham, Me., at a very early date in 1700, and
whose history of deep interest has been so carefully written by
De Alva Stanwood Alexander, Senator from Buffalo, N. Y. The
Clarks were one of the sturdiest families on that part of the
Maine coast. Captain David Perry and his wife were very
earnest Christians, and for many years she was a member of the
Baptist Church on Harpswell Neck. On the death of her husband she was left with six children, but she not only kept these

together and trained them to lives of great usefulness, but she became the friend and nurse of the sick people in the neighborhood, being ever willing to go early and late if she could help any person who was in suffering or need. She was a woman greatly beloved.

THE CHILDREN OF CAPTAIN DAVID PERRY AND JANE ALEXANDER

* * *

(7) ROSANNAH PERRY b. Oct., 1805; d. Boothbay, Me., Feb. 7, 1883; a woman of great energy and helpfulness of character; a faithful member of the Methodist Church; m. Capt. William Blake, b. Harpswell, Me., Sept. 13, 1799; d. at Boothbay, Me., where he and his family had lived for many years, June 5, 1878; the very successful Captain of fishing vessels; the son of Samuel Blake and Abigail Clark of Harpswell, Me.

(8) HANNAH STURTEVANT BLAKE b. Harpswell, Me., Jan. 11, 1823; d. at Bailey's Island, Me., Jan. 29, 1900; she and her husband were very helpful members of the Baptist Church; m. Jan. 18, 1864, Captain James Sinnett, Jr., b. July 9, 1825; d. March 26, 1909; Captain of several fishing vessels, and a good farmer at Bailey's Island, Me.; very faithful help in all religious work; the son of Capt. James Sinnett and Mary Johnson.

(9) CURTIS SUMNER SINNETT b. Aug. 1, 1876; d. in youth.

(8) CAPT. DAVID PERRY BLAKE b. Harpswell, Me., May 10, 1824; d. at Boothbay, Me., Apr. 19, 1870; a successful commander of fishing vessels; he and his wife were faithful members of the Methodist Episcopal Church; m. Oct. 8, 1849, Ann Barter, b. Barter's Island, Boothbay, Me., and d. Dec. 30, 1887 (63); the daughter of John Barter, Soldier of 1812 War; b. Oct. 31, 1794; m. Intent Oct. 12, 1816, to Susanna Fanly, b. Sept. 30, 1800; d. Dec. 6, 1872.

(9) SUSAN FRANCES BLAKE b. Aug. 31, 1853; resides Boothbay Harbor, Me.; Boothbay and Bath, Me., schools; Pythian Sister; m. (1st) Dec. 15, 1872, Levi Bradley Williams, b. Bath, Me.,

Nov. 6, 1847; d. Aug. 20, 1887; a very successful Cook; the son
of Isaiah Williams; m. (2d) Dec. 8, 1888, Edwin Lorenzo Giles;
b. Boothbay, Me., Nov. 6, 1847; Boothbay, Me., schools; Knight
of Pythias; a man of sterling qualities; truckman and paper
hanger at Boothbay Harbor, Me.; the son of William Giles and
Nancy Hutchings.

Children of the 1st marriage:

(10) HENRY FRANKOS WILLIAMS b. Apr. 11, 1874; an
engineer at Boothbay Harbor, Me.

(10) LILLIAN MAY WILLIAMS b. Sept. 28, 1878; resides
Boothbay Harbor, Me.; member of Pythian Sisters; m. May 13,
1907, Ralph Hayes Colby, b. Westport, Me., March 6, 1876;
Knight of Pythias; Chief Engineer on the Tug Boat, Fred E.
Richards of Rockland, Me., which is owned by the Rockland and
Rockport, Me., Lime Co., and tows barges from Rockland to
N. Y. City; he is the son of Christopher Columbus Colby and
Alzina ———

(11) FRANCES EDWINA COLBY b. Dec. 31, 1907.

(10) JENNIE PERRY WILLIAMS b. March 18, 1883; d. Jan. 1,
1909; "She had been Chief operator at the local Telephone
Exchange, Boothbay Harbor, Me., for over two years, performing her duties there in a very able and satisfactory manner. She
was a member of the Mizpah Temple Pythian Sisters, under
whose auspices her funeral services were held, assisted by Rev.
J. M. Shank of the M. E. Church and a quartet of her young
friends, Roy Rowe, Herbert Thurston, S. D. Stevens and Clark
Rowe. The floral offerings were many and beautiful, showing
clearly the great popularity of this most worthy young lady."

(10) ROSE ELLA WILLIAMS died at 2 1-2 years.

(10) ANNIE WILLIAMS died at eleven months.

(9) LOUISA JANE BLAKE b. Nov. 16, 1855; d. Oct. 14, 1873;
unm.

(9) ABBIE CORA BLAKE b. E. Boothbay, Me., Oct. 28, 1858;
resides Boothbay Harbor, Me.; of grand help in the completion
of this Perry History; studied in the schools of Boothbay and
Bath, Me.; m. Dec. 6, 1879, Justin Stevens Lewis, b. Bristol, Me.,
Oct. 20, 1855; a fine Cook on many large vessels; schools of
Damaricotta and Pemaquid, Me.; the son of Jacob Lewis and
Elizabeth Machaman, who resided in Pemaquid and Wiscassett,
Me.

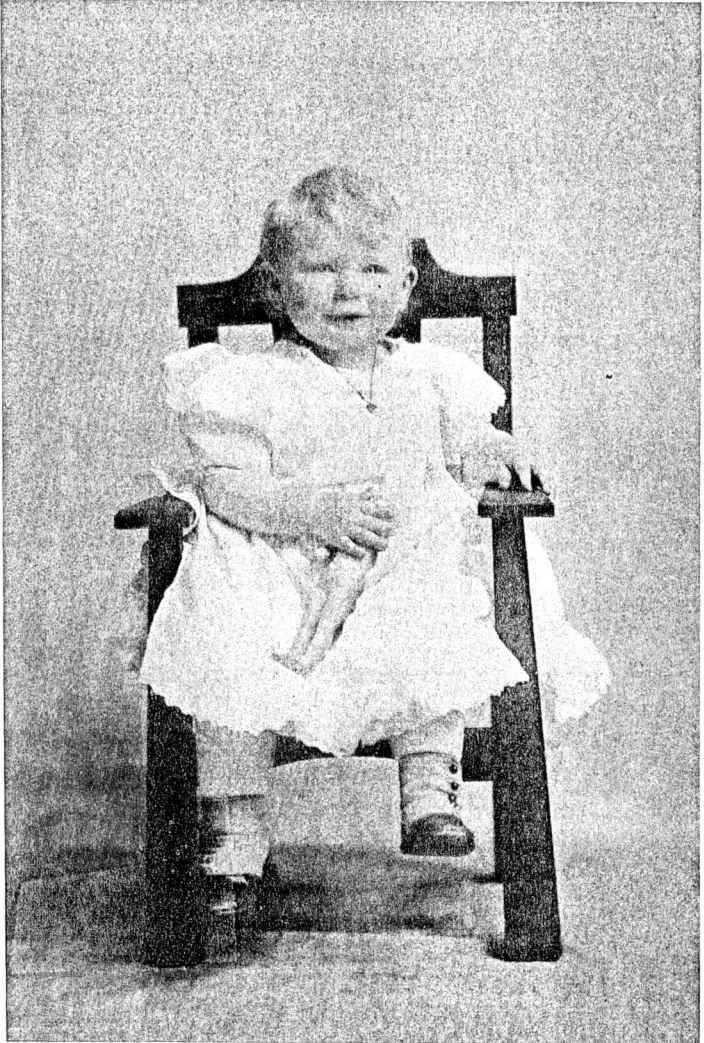

FRANCES EDWINA COLBY, B. DEC. 31, 1907

(10) ELMER LEWIS b. June 13, 1884; a very successful barber at Boothbay Harbor, Me.; unm.

(10) WALTER LEWIS b. June 13, 1886; d. Sept. 23, 1887.

(10) Child died in infancy.

(9) MARGARET ANN BLAKE b. E. Boothbay, Me., May 28, 1863; resides 22 York St., Bath, Me.; a faithful student in Boothbay, Me., schools; m. at Lowell, Mass., Jan. 1, 1894, Fred Chiever Carr, b. Bath, Me., Oct. 26, 1863; studied in Bath, Me., schools; tinsmith; Knight of Pythias; Free Mason; the son of John Carr and Rebecca ———, who resided in Dedham, Mass., and in Bath, Me.

(10) RUTH REBECCA CARR b. Mch. 12, 1897.

(8) ELIZABETH BLAKE b. Oct. 21, 1825; d. Boothbay, Me., Sept. 27, 1894 (69); a woman of noble qualities; studied in Boothbay, Me., schools; m. Nov. 28, 1847, Thomas Boyd Wylie, b. Boothbay, Me., Apr. 7, 1825; d. June 3, 1876; a fine blacksmith; the son of Robert Wylie and Jane Reed.

(9) HARRIET ELIZABETH WYLIE b. Oct. 2, 1848; d. Feb. 18, 1868.

(9) IZETTA WYLIE b. June 8, 1850; d. Apr. 24, 1893; she and her husband were excellent citizens of E. Boothbay, Me.; m. Mch. 14, 1873, Samuel Murray Seavey, b. Boothbay, Me., June 12, 1847; d. July 18, 1899; a very fine mechanic and ship carpenter; the son of James Seavey and Sarah Murray.

(10) FRED WILDER SEAVEY b. June 20, 1873; ship carpenter and proprietor of a boarding house at South Bristol, Me.; m. Nov. 3, 1897, Idella Clifford Thompson of Bristol, Me.

(11) DORRIS SEAVEY b. July, 1900.

(10) BENAIAH DOLLOFF SEAVEY b. E. Boothbay, Me., Apr. 3, 1875; an excellent sail maker at Boothbay Harbor, Me.; m. Mch. 4, 1903, Lillian Mabel Polland of Bristol, Me., b. Oct. 3, 1882; Bristol, Me., schools; the daughter of William Marcena Polland and Elva Jane—

(11) HAROLD LEROY SEAVEY b. July 7, 1903.

(11) MURIEL AUGUSTA SEAVEY b. Dec. 30, 1904.

(11) BENAIAH SEAVEY b. Jan. 27, 1908.

(10) EDWARD EVERETT SEAVEY b. Dec. 20, 1876; resides 12 Enfield St., Hartford, Conn.; boilermaker; m. Nina Hodgkins of Worcester, Mass. Children born at Worcester, Mass.

(11) RUTH ABBIE SEAVEY b. May 29, 1901.

(11) ROBERT EDWARD SEAVEY b. July 18, 1903.

(10) AUGUSTA GOUDY SEAVEY b. July 26, 1886; resides 12 Enfield St., Hartford, Conn.; schools of East Boothbay, Me., and of Worcester, Mass.

(9) CAPTAIN ALMOND LIBBY WYLIE b. East Boothbay, Me., Aug. 9, 1852; resides Newcastle, Me.; Captain of the coasting schooner, William H. Clifford; E. Boothbay schools; m. Aug. 27, 1879, Lizzie M. Chase of E. Boothbay, Me., b. Waterville, Me., Jan. 27, 1858; the daughter of George H. Chase, who m. in Waterville, Me., June 14, 1851, Joanna B. Tozier; these parents removed from Oakland, Me., to E. Boothbay, Me.

(10) Child died in infancy.

(9) NANCY JANE WYLIE b. Aug. 10, 1855; d. June 19, 1875.

(9) LECTINA WYLIE b. Aug. 27, 1858; d. Dec. 26, 1891; Boothbay, Me., schools; m. Dec. 6, 1875, Charles Ambrose Seavey, b. Aug. 17, 1838, d. Feb. 25, 1902; a successful contractor and builder; a brave soldier in the Civil War, Co. B, 45th Maine Regiment; served on the Monitor Monadnock; the son of James Seavey who was born at Kennebunk, Me., and of Sarah Murray.

(10) SARAH MURRAY SEAVEY b. E. Boothbay, Me., June 26, 1876; Boothbay, Me., schools; she and her husband are very faithful members of the Methodist Episcopal Church at East Boothbay, Me.; m. Dec. 7, 1897, Frank Clifton Adams of East Boothbay, Me.; b. July 18, 1874; studied in E. Boothbay, Me., schools and Bucksport, Me., Seminary; member of the firm of W. I. Adams & Co., shipbuilders, exceeding all others in that locality in work, having in March, 1905, celebrated the launching of their 105th vessel. The son of Wm. Irving Adams and Lydia A. Giles.

(11) ARTHUR MAHLON ADAMS b. June 21, 1898.

(11) FRANK IRVING ADAMS b. Feb. 8, 1900.

(11) RUTH VIRGINIA ADAMS b. June 24, 1902.

(11) PARKER SEAVEY ADAMS b. Sept. 27, 1904.

(11) ESTHER ADAMS b. Sept. 7, 1907.

(10) MARY LEICHMAN SEAVEY b. Nov. 16, 1878; Boothbay, Me., schools; in winter an operator in the machine hall of the Westboro, Mass., Hat Co.; spends the summers with her sister, Mrs. Adams.

(10) CHARLES BRECK SEAVEY b. E. Boothbay, Me., Sept. 10, 1890; graduated from E. Boothbay, Me., High School, June 18, 1907; unm.

(9) ANNIE MARY WYLIE b. Oct. 22, 1861, d. Aug. 1, 1887; m. in Boston, Mass., Jan. 14, 1885, Harvey Dwight Bodwell, b. Boston, Mass., Dec. 10, 1862; resides 40 Willow Ave., Somerville, Mass.; he and his wife were attendants at the Walnut Ave. Congregational Church, Roxbury, Mass.; he is salesman for the Lord Baltimore Press; graduated from Boston, Mass., schools; the son of Chas. Horace Bodwell and Mary Data; the father was born Weston, Mass.; carpenter; graduated from Boston, Mass., Grammar School.

(10) MARY ELIZABETH BODWELL b. Boston, Mass., July 15, 1888; stenographer in her father's office; graduated from Somerville, Mass., English High School, June, 1906; attends Somerville, Mass., Baptist Church.

(9) EDWARD WYLIE b. Mch. 21, 1864, d. Feb. 23, 1900; m. Aug. 9, 1891, in Stockton, Calif., Emeline Peters Nichols b. Sept. 28, 1869; she was educated in the Stockton, Calif., schools and Business College, and in St. Agnes Academy of Stockton; she was the daughter of John Nichols, who was engaged in the wholesale furniture business, and of Desdemonia Tayler. Mrs. Emeline P. Wylie m. (2d) in Reading, Mass., 1900, George E. Gill; her address is North Eastham, Mass., Box 6; son of her second marriage, Edwards Nichols Gill, a very fine scholar. Her second husband, Mr. Gill, has a fine asparagus farm.

(10) THOMAS BOYD WYLIE b. June 12, 1894; d. July 16, 1895.

(10) HATTIE MAY WYLIE b. June 1, 1896; d. Jan. 15, 1897.

(10) ETHEL GERTRUDE WYLIE b. Mch. 26, 1898; d. Feb. 15, 1899.

(9) EVERTS McQUESTION WYLIE b. July 3, 1868; salesman; unm.

(8) CHARLOTTE PARSONS BLAKE b. Boothbay, Me., Nov. 1, 1827; d. Dec. 3, 1901; she and her husband highly respected citizens of Boothbay, Me.; m. Feb. 24, 1852, Eliphalet Holbrook b. Sept. 18, 1824; d. April 3, 1905; a very successful trader for many years at Linnekin's Neck, Boothbay, Me.; History of Boothbay, Me.; "To this man belongs the distinction of being the merchant over the longest term of years of any ever in our town. He commenced the grocery trade in 1845, and in 1905 he still retains an interest in this business, and gives some attention to it." He was the son of Ezekiel Holbrook and Dorcas Farnham.

(9) ALDEN GRIMES HOLBROOK b. Oct. 17, 1852; a very successful storekeeper at Linnekin's Neck, Boothbay, Me.; graduate(

from Lincoln Academy, Damariscotta, Me.; m. Dec. 23, 1878, Abbie Eliza Martin of Boothbay, Me.; b. Nov. 4, 1856; the daughter of George A. Martin and Mary J. Farnham.

(10) EZEKIEL MARTIN HOLBROOK b. May 20, 1883; fisherman.

(10) RUTH ELLEN HOLBROOK b. Nov. 4, 1893; graduated from East Boothbay, Me., High School.

(9) ELLEN DORCAS HOLBROOK b. Jan. 20, 1858; m. Oct. 31, 1882, Jainus Prentiss Jones of Jefferson, Me., b. Nobleboro, Me., Feb. 8, 1846; graduated at Eastman's Business College, Poughkeepsie, N. Y.; teacher and bookkeeper; the son of Prentiss Jones and Clara Hall of Nobleboro, Me.

(10) CLARA BELL JONES b. Oct. 30, 1885.

(10) ELIPHALET PRENTISS JONES b. July 23, 1900.

(9) ORRA ANN HOLBROOK b. Jan. 27, 1865; m. Jan. 26, 1898, George Webster Martin of Boothbay, Me., b. Mch. 21, 1865; resides Linnekin's Neck, Me.; the son of George A. Martin and Mary J. Farnham; no children.

(8) JANE PERRY BLAKE b. Nov. 23, 1829, d. Boothbay Harbor, Me., Jan. 23, 1896; unm.

(8) CAPTAIN LEVI BLAKE b. Oct. 11, 1831; has resided at East Boothbay, Me., for some time; the very successful Captain of several large fishing vessels. On Aug. 14, 1864, his schooner, Restless, was sunk by the Rebel Privateer Tallahassee. In May, 1888, he removed from Boothbay, Me., to Chelsea, Mass., and held several fine positions with firms in Boston, Mass.; m. Mch. 5, 1863, Sarah Jane Reed, b. Boothbay, Me., May 23, 1836; a woman of noble and helpful character; the daughter of Levi S. Reed and Abigail Curtis Perry.

(9) Morrill L. Blake b. July 18, 1867; resides E. Boothbay, Me.; for some years was a very successful Engineer in a Power House at New Haven, Conn.; m. May 24, 1894, Eva Williams, who d. Aug. 2, 1899; no children.

(9) LESTER PERRY BLAKE b. Oct. 4, 1869; employed in the wholesale hardware store at No. 80 Washington St., Boston, Mass.; m. July 20, 1895, Clara L. McDougall b. Boothbay, Me., May 27, 1869; the daughter of James McDougall and Lizzie Dolloff.

(10) HAZEL CROCKETT BLAKE b. Aug. 23, 1897; a very fine scholar.

(10) THURBER BLAKE b. Dec. 2, 1900; d. June 28, 1900.

(10) FOREST REED BLAKE b. June 25, 1903.

(10) MARIAN BLAKE b. Nov. 24, 1907.

(8) WILLIAM TWOMBLY BLAKE b. July 14, 1833; d. in youth.

(8) RUFUS MURRAY BLAKE b. Dec. 23, 1835, d. May 11, 1870; mariner; m. Jan. 7, 1857, Aldana Linnekin b. Boothbay, Me., Jan. 3, 1841; the daughter of James Linnekin and Abigail Pratt (she m. (2d) Dec. 24, 1888, William M. Sawyer.)

(9) LYNDA FRANCES BLAKE b. Oct. 17, 1866; resides Portland, Me.; m. Dec. 18, 1887, Charles W. Fuller; machinist.

(10) RUFUS WOODBURY FULLER b. Feb. 14, 1888.

(10) ELLERY ANDERSON FULLER b. Feb. 4, 1893.

(8) CHARLES CUSHMAN BLAKE b. Oct. 11, 1837, d. in the Spring of 1903; resided at South Bend, Washington, for some years; m. Jan. 12, 1874, Ruth Augusta Montgomery of Boothbay, Me.; the daughter of Andrew R. Montgomery and Ruth Seavey.

(9) ISABELLA M. BLAKE b. Apr. 5, 1875; m. Apr. 15, 1899, John T. Welsh.

(9) ALBERT N. LEWIS BLAKE b. Apr. 29, 1877.

(8) MARY FRANCES BLAKE b. Feb. 10, 1845; d. Oct. 22, 1910; resided Boothbay Harbor, Me.; a woman of noble and helpful character; faithful member of M. E. Church 40 years; studied in Boothbay, Me., schools; m. (1st) Dec. 28, 1865, Benaiah Preston Dolloff b. Boothbay, Me., Aug. 26, 1842, d. Dec. 28, 1880; a very brave soldier in the Civil War; Lt. in Co. K, 19th Maine Regiment; after the Civil War he was engaged in the livery business; the son of Benaiah Dolloff and Clarissa Veasey. M. (2d) Apr. 28, 1887, Alonzo Perry Wylie b. Boothbay, Me., June 25, 1843; a barber at Boothbay Harbor, Me.; in the one shop for over twenty years; has just taken a new shop; he was formerly employed in the Boot and Shoe business; he is a man of fine executive ability; he has filled the office of Chancellor Commander in the Knights of Pythias; in the year 1890 Mr. Wylie served as First Selectman for the unexpired term of Joseph Maddocks; has served on the Board of Health for several years; he is the son of John Wylie and Adeline Lewis. He and his wife are members of the Methodist Church. Children of the first marriage of Mary Frances Blake b. Boothbay Harbor, Me.

(9) GRACE AMES DOLLOFF b. Dec. 11, 1867; resides Boothbay Harbor, Me.; attends the Methodist Church; schools of Boothbay Harbor, Me.; m. Jan. 18, 1886, Capt. George Beaman

McLellan b. W. Boothbay Harbor, Me., Oct. 3, 1862; a very successful Captain; the son of Randall McLellan, who is deceased,
and of Sarah Emeline Wylie of W. Boothbay Harbor.

(10) FRANCES McLELLAN b. Sept. 1, 1887; Chief Operator
at Boothbay Harbor, Me., New England Telephone and Tele-
graph Company.

(10) RICHARD McLELLAN b. Aug. 18, 1900.

(9) SHERBURN RUFUS DOLLOFF b. May 20, 1870; a barber at
Boothbay Harbor, Me.; he and his wife are members of the
Methodist Church; Son of Veterans, Free Mason and Knight of
Pythias; m. June 22, 1903, Lillian Maria Walker b. Worcester,
Mass., Feb. 26, 1867; Pythian Sister.   She is President of Meth-
odist Ladies' Aid Society; the daughter of Asa V. Walker and
Caroline Elizabeth Lewis.

(9) MOSES PRESTON DOLLOFF b. May 14, 1879; member of
the M. A. Perkins Grocery Firm, Boothbay Harbor, Me.; Free
Mason and Knight of Pythias; graduated from East Boothbay,
Me., High School, June 18, 1895; he and his wife attend the
Methodist Church; m. May 3, 1905, Mary Richards Hodgdon b. E.
Boothbay, Me., Apr. 11, 1877; graduated from E. Boothbay, Me.,
High School, 1895; the daughter of Silas Lee Hodgdon and Car
oline Wheaton.

(10) SILAS BENAIAH DOLLOFF b. July 22, 1906.

(10) CAROLINE FRANCES DOLLOFF b. Jan. 22, 1908.

Child of the second marriage of Mary Frances (Blake) Dolloff, with Alonzo Perry Wylie.

(9) MARY ALICE WYLIE b. Feb. 8, 1888; graduated from the
Boothbay Harbor, Me., High School, June, 1906; a very successful teacher for two years; member of Pythian Sisters.

* * *

(7) LUCY PERRY, the second child of Captain David Perry, b
Dec. 22, 1806, d. at North Yarmouth, Me., Sept. 28, 1870 (64);
a woman of noble helpfulness in the home and in all the neighborhoods where she lived; m. William Twombly of Gorham, Me.,
who d. at N. Yarmouth, Me., Mch. 2, 1868 (68-9); he was a man
of sturdy qualities, and had a wonderful gift as an interesting
relater of stories of the olden times; descended from one of the
strongest of old New England families; their happy home will
long be remembered by many people.

(8) TWINS died in infancy.

(8) ELIZA TWOMBLY d. in childhood.

(8) JABEZ CUSHMAN TWOMBLY b. Gorham, Me., Feb. 27, 1844, d. at N. Yarmouth, Me., Dec. 17, 1870 (30) a very industrious shoemaker at N. Yarmouth, Me. He was a young man of great promise.

(8) HENRY E. TWOMBLY b. Mechanics Falls, Me., Feb. 27, 1844, d. Newton Center, Mass., July 7, 1909; he was a very efficient business man of Boston, Mass., entering the employ of the firm of Coleman, Mead & Co., when about eighteen years of age; the firm name was changed to Langley, Burr & Co.; and of this firm he was a very efficient member for thirty-one years; he and his wife were members of the Unitarian Church at Newton Centre, Mass.; he became a member of the Tyrian Lodge of Free Masons in Mch., 1864; Wm. P. Preble, Grand Master. M. Jan. 1, 1872, Carrie Maria Miller, b. in Belfast, Me., Nov. 7, 1849; resides Newton Centre, Mass.; the daughter of Justus Gorham Miller, a California miner of 1849; and of Olivia Maria Lewis of Belfast, Me.

(9) LENA MILLER TWOMBLY b. Nov. 9, 1874; resides Newton Centre, Mass. Graduated from Chauncey Hall School, Boston, Mass.; and from Emerson School of Oratory, Boston, Mass.; unm.

(9) FRED HENRY TWOMBLY b. Somerville, Mass., Apr. 19, 1876; 60 Laight St., N. Y. City., N. Y., graduated from Chauncy Hall School, Boston, Mass., June, 1894; from the Mass. Institute of Technology, Boston, Mass., June, 1898. Manager of the Foreign Department of R. E. Dietz Company, Lantern Manufacturers, 60 Laight St., N. Y. City, largest lantern makers in the world; m. June 18, 1903, Ethelberta Hasbrook b. Cillicothe, Missouri, July 31, 1876; graduated from Wellesley College, 1895; the daughter of Charles Electus Hasbrook and Delia Elkins of Galesburg, Ill.

(10) FRED HASBROOK TWOMBLY b. July 24, 1904, d. Aug. 9, 1904.

(9) GEORGE COLEMAN TWOMBLY b. Boston, Mass., Oct. 18, 1883; graduated from Newton Centre High School; from Harvard College, 1906; Agriculturist at Hudson, Mass.; unm.

(8) FRANCES CUSHMAN TWOMBLY b. Aug. 15, 1849, d. at Buxton, Me., 1879; a very bright and cheery Christian woman,

beloved by all who knew her; m. John O. Harris of N. Yarmouth, Me., and soon after removed to Buxton, Me., where he was employed in a prominent position in a large sawmill; no children.

* * *

(7) ABIGAIL CURTIS PERRY, the third child of Capt. David Perry, b. Bailey's Island, Harpswell, Me., June 12, 1809, d. Boothbay, Me., Aug. 4, 1883; a woman of noblest Christian character and constantly doing good to all around her and to those in distant places by her letters filled with Christian hope and cheer; m. Dec. 2, 1830, Levi Shattuck Reed b. Westport, Me., Oct. 27, 1803, d. at East Boothbay, Me., July 13, 1885 (83—3 m.); he removed to Boothbay, Me., when he was quite a young man; for many years a very successful ship carpenter, and known far and wide for his honest work and dealings; he went to California in 1849 and remained there 3½ years. He and his wife were very faithful and helpful members of the Methodist Church at E. Boothbay, Me. He settled in E. Boothbay, 1833. The son of George Reed, a farmer at Woolwich, Me., where he died Nov. 6, 1836 (66); a man of noble character; m. in Edgecomb, Me., 1794, Sarah Shattuck, b. Georgetown, Me., June 5, 1777, d. Woolwich, Me., Jan. 23, 1808.

(8) JOHN PERRY REED b. Dec. 10, 1832, d. June 11, 1906. A carpenter and always lived in E. Boothbay, Me.; member of the Methodist Church; m. Jan. 21, 1856, Julia E. Blake; resides E. Boothbay, Me.; b. July 27, 1833; the daughter of Samuel Blake and Martha Hutchings.

(9) JULIA FANNIE REED b. Sept. 18, 1857; m. 1876, Zina Webber b. Oct. 5, 1854; the son of James Webber and Julia Perkins.

(10) JAMES Z. WEBBER b. June 10, 1877; a private in Spanish American War, 1898.

(10) FRANK B. WEBBER b. Nov. 16, 1879; private in the Spanish American War.

(10) LEVI REED WEBBER b. Dec. 1, 1882.

(10) LIZZIE M. WEBBER b. Oct. 16, 1884.

(10) FANNIE ETHEL WEBBER b. Feb. 17, 1887.

(9) LIZZIE A. REED b. May 5, 1862; m. Jan. 23, 1884, Henry M. Fuller.

(9) WALTER REED b. Sept. 26, 1867, d. Sept. 21, 1870.

(9) GILMAN (GILBERT) REED b. Nov. 21, 1872; blacksmith; m. 1895, Annie Sargent of Boothbay Harbor, Me.

(10) SON.

(8) GEORGE REED b. July 26, 1834; d. May 4, 1907. He was a house carpenter at Chelsea, Mass., for many years; a member of the Odd Fellows; an attendant at the Methodist Church; m. Dec. 7, 1860, Mary Abigail Race b. Boothbay, Me., May 12, 1841; the daughter of Captain John Race; resides Orange St., Chelsea, Mass.

(9) LETTIE STROUT REED b. Sept. 30, 1861, d. Nov. 11, 1884; unm.

(9) ELLA FRANCES REED b. April 30, 1870, d. April 15, 1893.

(8) SARAH JANE REED b. May 23, 1856; resides E. Boothbay, Me.; m. Levi Blake. Full records under Levi Blake.

(8) MARGARET PERRY REED b. Aug. 19, 1839; resides with her son Dr. Eugene Wylie, 16 River St., Dorchester Lower Mills, Dorchester, Mass.; resided at 59 Cottage St., Chelsea, Mass., for many years; having moved there Oct. 3, 1870; m. Dec. 29, 1864, Charles Wylie, b. Boothbay, Me., Sept. 1, 1829, d. at the home of his son, Dr. Wylie, Dorchester, Mass., Aug. 24, 1909; Obituary in the Boston, Mass., Globe: "For forty years Charles Wylie was one of Chelsea's most prominent citizens. At the time of his retirement from work two years ago, he was one of the oldest builders in active service in Boston. His grandfather Wylie was one of the founders of Boothbay, Me., and in that place Charles Wylie learned his trade as a carpenter, and a little later engaged in building operations in Damariscotta, twelve miles away, walking back and forth to his work each day. He built the Congregational Church in Boothbay, which is now the property of the Baptist Church. At the outbreak of the Civil War he enlisted in the 43d Mass. Volunteers. At the close of the War he settled in Boston, starting in the building business at 5 Jackson Place in 1870. He resided in Chelsea for forty years and lost all his possessions in the great fire in that city. At the time when the building was razed to make room for the Parker House he had the contract. He also remodelled the Burnham Building on Tremont St. In Chelsea he was prominent in the cause of no-license. He was a Trustee of the Old Ladies' Home Asso. and the First Baptist Church of Chelsea. At one time he was Treasurer and Steward of the M. E. Bellingham Church of Chelsea. He was a member of Post 35, G. A. R., of Chelsea. He was a noble and faith-

ful Christian. He was the son of Robert Wylie and Jane Webber." Mr. and Mrs. Charles Wylie were widely known for their
generous hospitality and helpfulness, and for their sturdy and
cheery aid to scores of people. Their names, deeds, and words
will long be remembered.

(9) CLARENCE D. WYLIE b. Apr. 17, 1866, d. Dec. 26, 1871.

(9) PARKER REED WYLIE b. Jan. 3, 1868; resides 16 Green-
brier St., Dorchester, Mass.; graduated from Williams School,
Chelsea, Mass., 1885; master mechanic, conducting a very pros-
perous business; m. July 7, 1892, Clara B. Fox, b. Farmingdale,
Me., Feb. 22, 1870; graduated from Shurtleff School, Chelsea,
Mass., 1885; the daughter of Wm. T. Fox and Annie Landers
Johnson of Farmingdale, Me.

(10) ROBERT JOHNSON WYLIE b. Thursday, Dec. 28, 1893.

(10) RUSSELL REED WYLIE b. Dec. 28, 1893, d. Sept. 13,
1895.

(10) ROLAND SHATTUCK WYLIE b. Friday, Jan. 24, 1897.

(10) RUTH REED WYLIE b. Jan. 24, 1897.

(10) EFFIE MARGARET WYLIE b. July 21, 1901.

(9) EMMONS KILBY WYLIE b. Dec. 27, 1869; resides 68 High
St., Malden, Mass.; graduated from Williams School, Chelsea,
Mass., 1886; wholesale hats, caps, and straw goods, Boston,
Mass.; a faithful workman; m. Jan. 15, 1896, Mabel E. Tatten b.
Boston, Mass., Mch. 28, 1870; graduated from Shurtleff School,
Chelsea, Mass., 1887; the daughter of George Francis Tatten and
Susan Frances Horn of Boston, Mass.

(10) EMMONS FRANCIS WYLIE b. May 25, 1897.

(10) EDGAR NELSON WYLIE b. May 17, 1901.

(9) DR. EUGENE CUSHMAN WYLIE b. Sept. 3, 1872; resides
556 Washington St., Dorchester Center, Mass.; graduated from
the Williams School, and High School, Chelsea, Mass.; and from
Harvard Medical School, 1894; diploma 1895; a very successful
physician; m. Oct. 27, 1897, Bertha G. Hastings b. St. Johnsbury,
Vt., Dec. 12, 1874; graduated from the Shurtleff School and High
School, Chelsea, Mass.; the daughter of Bela Stone Hastings of
Lyman, N. H., and of Amelia Caroline Babcock of Burke, Vt.;
these parents resided in St. Johnsbury, Vt., and in Chelsea, Mass.

(10) GERTRUDE CUSHMAN WYLIE b. Sept. 21, 1910.

(9) FRED SMART WYLIE b. Sept. 29, 1874; resides 132 Brom-
field St., Wollaston, Mass.; a man of sterling qualities; graduated from Schools of Chelsea and Boston, Mass.; stock broker;

m. Aug. 4, 1904, Harriet Ellen Plummer b. South Presque Isle, Me., Dec. 22, 1879; graduated from Williams School, Chelsea, Mass.; daughter of Julius Augustus Plummer who d. Feb. 1, 1904, and of Ida May Sprague, who resides Laconia, N. H.

(10) DALLAS WYLIE b. Chelsea, Mass., Sept. 3, 1905.

(10) ELIOT WYLIE b. Boston, Mass., June 27, 1909.

(9) ARTHUR WEBBER PERRY WYLIE b. Nov. 21, 1882; graduated form Chelsea, Mass. High School; studied in Dartmouth College; now a student in Nashotah, Wis., Episcopal Seminary.

(8) HARRIET NEWELL REED b. Jan. 14, 1840; d. Aug. 17, 1841.

(8) LEVI SHATTUCK REED b. Aug. 17, 1841; d. Nov. 10, 1905. "He was a life-long resident of East Boothbay, Me. In the early part of his life he followed the sea for about fifteen years, but after his marriage he worked with his father, and for many years he was a very successful carpenter and shipbuilder. He afterwards formed a co-partnership under the firm name, L. S. Reed & Co., carrying a complete line of furniture and also establishing an undertaking department. Although this co-partnership was dissolved some time ago, Mr. Reed still carried on the furniture and undertaking business up to the time of his last sickness. One of the principal features of his entire course of life was exactness and honesty in all his dealings. Those who patronized him in business had every confidence in him. He was a member of the Bay View Lodge of Free Masons. He was also a member of the Knights of Pythias. During the last days of his sickness the Pythian emblem seemed ever before him. The interment was in the family lot at Boothbay Center, where the Pythians took full charge of the services." M. Dec. 24, 1867, Marcia Elizabeth S. Farnham b. Boothbay, Me., Jan. 31, 1843; with whom Mr. Reed spent thirty years of uninterrupted happiness. She was the daughter of John Farnham and Dorcas Sargent. She resides at E. Boothbay, Me.; no children.

(8) MARY ALICE REED b. Sept. 11, 1847; d. at Rockland, Me., Sept. 23, 1875; m. Dec. 25, 1866, Joseph Woodbury Davis, who died in the spring of 1907; he was Aide to Gen. Tilson in 1861; a man of noble character; the proprietor of the well-known restaurant on Tilson's Wharf, Rockland, Me. "Mrs. Davis had been ill only a few days, so that her sudden death was a great surprise to all. She was one of the most estimable women of Rockland, Me.,

and was well and widely known in the community, being a member of the Edwin Libby Ladies' Relief Corps, and of the Golden Rod Chapter of the Order of the Eastern Star, and her friends are almost countless, and hold her in the highest esteem and warmest regard. Her qualities of mind and heart, her genial, happy disposition, her self-sacrifice in behalf of others, her sympathy with suffering wherever she saw it, her charity and helpfulness towards the needy, and her readiness to do and give for any and every good work; were such that it was impossible to be drawn into intimate relations with her and not love her. Rev. C. W. Bradlee officiated at the funeral and the interment was in the Achorn Cemetery, Rockland, Me."

(9) ELMER NEY DAVIS b. Nov. 21, 1868; salesman in New York City.

(9) ELIZABETH TILSON DAVIS b. Mch., 1870; resides Boston, Mass.; m. Mch. 7, 1892, Thomas C. Fales of Rockland, Me.; Manager of The Adams Express Co., Boston, Mass.

(10) CRAWFORD FALES b. Jan. 10, 1895.

* * *

(7) REV. JOHN CURTIS PERRY b. Bailey's Island, Me., Dec. 25, 1813; d. Mch. 20, 1880. Early in life he became a very faithful Christian He was admitted to the Maine Methodist Episcopal Conference at Hallowell, Maine, on trial, June 27, 1837; and for over forty years he was one of the most faithful ministers of New England. He had twenty-six appointments, among these being Rockland, Bucksport, Searsport, Saco, and the Congress Street Church, Portland, Me. In all his parishes many souls were led to the Master. He was appointed to several of his fields of labor several times, among these to his native town of Harpswell, Me., which was always so dear to his heart. His long ministerial record was marked by great ability and extraordinary faithfulness. He m. Jan. 14, 1841, Mary E. Baston, b. Hiram, Me., Nov. 2, 1820; d. at Peak's Island, Me., Dec. 2, 1893; she was a woman of great ability, and of true faith and purity of character; the daughter of Loammi Baston and Rebecca Powers of Saco, Me.

(8) HIRAM PERRY b. Bucksprt, Me., 1842; d. in infancy.

(8) FREDERICK PERRY b. Standish, Me., and died in infancy.

(8) JOHN SOMERFIELD PERRY b. Rockland, Me., Nov. 30,

1845; resides 105 Grant St., Portland, Me.; a man of earnest character; the writer of many fine poems; m. Sept. 24, 1871, Arabella H. Clark of South Paris, Me., who died in that town, July, 1873 (25 years.).

(9) ELMER F. PERRY b. Sep. 10, 1872; d. Gorham, Me., May, 1874.

(8) ALBION ATWOOD PERRY b. Standish, Me., Jan. 26, 1851; resides 5 Foster St., Somerville, Mass.; educated in the schools of Standish and Monmouth, Me.; graduated from Monmouth, Me., Academy and from the Mass. College of Pharmacy. He was a student of fine ability. "When Mr. Perry was but eighteen years old he entered a drug store at Somerville, Mass., and, while not intending to remain there permanently, he did his work thoroughly, for this has been characteristic of his whole life. After a few years he entered the Law School of the Boston University, and after finishing his course he opened an office in Somerville, Mass. Affairs prospered with him, and in 1886 he formed a partnership with Hon. S. Z. Bowman. Though not a politician, in the accepted sense of the word, Mr. Perry has often been called to public offices by the vote of his townsmen. In the middle seventies he was elected to the School Board. Later he was in the Common Council, the Board of Aldermen, and the Water Board. In 1895 he was nominated as the citizens' candidate for Mayoralty, and was elected. He was re-elected in 1896 and 1897. And so well pleased with his administration were his fellow-citizens that would he have accepted it, he would have been named for the fourth term. He did not feel that the state of his health admitted of his serving again. The esteem in which Mr. Perry was held is shown by the following endorsement of his candidacy which appeared in the Somerville, Mass., Journal; 'The Committee of two hundred acted wisely we think in choosing Mr. Perry as their candidate; undoubtedly he is the strongest and best qualified man they could have accepted. A sound business man, and a lawyer, he has a wide experience in dealing with Somerville affairs as a member of the Common Council, school committee, water board, and through his connection with local banking institutions. His scholarly culture, his eloquence as a public speaker, and the fact that he represents no clique, or faction, and never has, are all elements in his favor. In his capacity as a private citizen, as well as during the years when he was in office, he has been alive to the best interests of the City, always

taking an active part in furthering its welfare. Mr. Perry is con-
scientious and painstaking, and, as we said last week, is an ideal
candidate.'" Another leading journal has well said, "As President of the Somerville, Mass., Bank, Mr. Perry did much to
strengthen that institution, and during his office the Bank had a
wonderful growth. As Mayor he was a very efficient man. His
business life has been spent in Somerville, and he understood the
needs of the City and conscientiously performed his duty. He
gave his undivided attention to his work, and retired from his
office meriting the approbation of the citizens. He is a man of
ability and sterling qualities, well-known for his integrity and
good judgment, and is a popular speaker in much demand at public gatherings. Maine may justly be proud of her son; Somerville is glad to claim him as a citizen." Mr. Perry m. (1st) Dec.
31, 1874, Mary Ellen Brooks b. Charlestown, Mass., Oct. 26,
1852; d. Jan. 9, 1904; graduated from Charlestown, Mass., High
School, and was a woman of noble qualities; the daughter of John
Brooks, Esq., and Hannah W. Dana. M. (2d) Apr. 11, 1907,
Virginia Blair Means b. Steubenville, Ohio, Apr. 20, 1857; the
daughter of Judge Thomas Means and Annie Stewart; a noble
woman. No children by either marriage.

(8) JASON BASTON PERRY b. Saco, Me., Nov. 9, 1853; resides
Leeds Centre, Me.; Superintendent of Corn Canning Factories
for many years; a man of great executive ability and faithfulness; Knight of Pythias; m. Feb. 25, 1885, Edith Grey Haskell
b. West Poland, Me., Jan. 29, 1861; a woman of great helpfulness; the daughter of H. G. O. Haskell and Meredith Scribner,
who resided at Poland and Otisfield, Me.; no children.

(8) FRANK LINCOLN PERRY b. Standish, Me., Nov. 26, 1861;
for some time traveling agent for a large type-manufacturing
Company, and resided at Portland, Me.; m. Dec. 24, 1884, Gertrude E. Williston of Portland, Me.

(9) RALPH WILLIAMSON PERRY b. Jan. 5, 1886.

(9) HAROLD FRANKLIN PERRY b. July 22, 1890; d. Chelsea
Mass., Feb. 9, 1892.

(9) FRANK CLIFTON PERRY b. Chelsea, Mass., July 25, 1892.

* * *

(7) MARGARET PHILLBROOK PERRY, fifth child of Captain
David Perry, b. Jan. 8, 1816; d. July 12, 1902; always resided at
Bailey's Island, Me.; m. Nov. 6, 1838, Captain Hugh Sinnett, 2d,

b. Bailey's Island, Me., Oct. 27, 1814, d. April 2, 1907; a successful Captain of fishing vessels and a California miner, 1852 and 1853; the son of Captain James Sinnett and Mary Johnson.

(8) CAPTAIN DAVID PERRY SINNETT b. Bailey's Island, Me., Oct. 19, 1843; merchant, fish dealer and Postmaster at Bailey's Island; m. (1st) April 22, 1867, Mary Caroline Alexander b. Bailey's Island, Me., Oct. 16, 1840, d. Aug. 25, 1886; the daughter of David Perry Alexander and Finette Greenleaf of Boothbay, Me. M. (2d) Mrs. Almira S. Johnson.

Children of the first marriage:

(9) Chester B. Sinnett b. Feb. 12, 1868; fisherman at Bailey's Island; m. Mch. 24, 1892, Jennie S. Stetson b. Livermore, Me., July 17, 1865; the daughter of William M. Stetson and Eliza Jane Merrill.

(10) CHESTER MAXIM SINNETT b. Jan. 19, 1900.

(10) CHARLES PERRY SINNETT b. Nov. 16, 1901.

(9) HERBERT PERRY SINNETT b. Oct. 30, 1870; fisherman at Bailey's Island, Me.; m. Sept. 24, 1893, Mrs. Bessie D. Potter of Hallowell, Me., b. W. Gardiner, Me., Sept. 9, 1864; daughter of John Gould Baker and widow of Mr. Potter.

(10) EFFIE MILDRED SINNETT b. June 12, 1896.

(9) MAGGIE BELLE SINNETT b. Mch. 30, 1874; d. Dec. 3, 1880.

(9) MAGGIE E. SINNETT b. April 29, 1882; resides Bailey's Island, Me.; studied in Westbrook, Me., Seminary; m. July 7, 1900, Claude Russell Johnson b. Bailey's Island, Me., Dec. 17, 1878; fisherman; the son of Capt. Elisha C. Johnson and Gustina O. Bibber.

(10) VILERA BELLE JOHNSON b. Mch. 14, 1902.

(10) PARKER RUSSELL JOHNSON b. Jan. 18, 1906.

(10) CLARITA LOUISE JOHNSON b. Aug. 30, 1908.

(8) REV. CHARLES NELSON SINNETT b. May 31, 1847; studied in North Yarmouth Academy, Yarmouth, Me.; graduated from Bangor, Me., Theological Seminary, June 1874; ordained as a Congregational minister at Lebanon, Me., May 31, 1875; has been pastor of several Congregational Churches in New England and the West; has contributed in prose and verse to all the leading religious papers of the country; author of "The Norsk

Gopher," and other books; has published several Church and family histories.

* * *

(7) ALICE REED PERRY, the sixth child of Capt. David Perry, b. Mch. 12, 1817, d. at Webster, Me., Aug. 7, 1865. Early in life she united with the Harpswell, Me., Baptist Church, and throughout her life was a very devoted Christian, a fine Bible student, a loving and patient wife and mother, and beloved by all her neighbors. After her marriage she united by letter with the West Bowdoin, Me., Free Baptist Church. M. Sept. 25, 1848, William Totmau Higgins b. Lisbon, Me., Feb. 19, 1826; now resides with his daughter, Mrs. Wagg, at Bowdoinham, Me. When a young man he united with the West Bowdoin, Me., Free Baptist Church, and has been a very faithful Christian, and of great help in all the neighborhoods where he has lived. He became Deacon of the Church in 1876; and continued to hold that office in a very worthy manner until obliged to resign it on account of ill health. He was a very successful farmer. The son of Zaccheus Higgins and Betsy Totman; grandson of Dyer Higgins and Susan Smith, and thus descended from some of the studiest old Maine families.

(8) MATILDA JANE HIGGINS b. Webster, Me., Oct. 20, 1850, d. May 25, 1875; she was baptized in the West Bowdoin, Me., Free Baptist Church in her fifteenth year by Rev. Mark Getchell, and was a very helpful Christian in all places where she lived; she was a constant attendant at Church, no matter what the weather might be; and the people often said that her face shining with the Master's love was a constant benediction to them. Her letters full of hope and cheer went winging their way to many nooks and corners of the world. After her marriage she united by letter with the Pine Street Free Baptist Church of Lewiston, Me. M. Oct. 16, 1873, Israel Folsom b. Strong, Me., Oct. 16, 1852; resides 38 Nichols St., Lewiston, Me.; he was baptized in the First Baptist Church of Lewiston, Me., by Rev. Dr. William Tecumseh Chase in his twenty-fourth year, and afterwards united by letter with the Court St. Baptist Church of Auburn, Me. A man of the most sturdy and trustworthy character, and deeply interested in all good causes and historical matters. He is a Master Mason in the Rabboni Lodge No. 150, of Lewiston, Me. His line of the Folsom Family is: (1) John Folsom, the immigrant; (2) Israel Folsom, the second son; (3) Israel Folsom; (4)

Israel Folsom;(5) Benjamin Folsom; (6) Daniel Folsom who
married Martha Quimby; (7) William Quimby Folsom of Industry, Me., and a brave soldier in the Civil War; m. Mary Stevens
Phillips. (8) Israel Folsom.

(9) Twin sons b. Lewiston, Me., Apr. 20, 1875; one of whom
died in infancy.

(9) WILLIAM HIGGINS FOLSOM b. Apr. 20, 1875; resides 17
Grant St., Burlington, Vt.; graduated from Burlington, Vt., High
School, 1897; from Ste Martine College, Canada, 1901, with the
highest honors; holds a Teacher's Diploma from the French
Academy of the United States, N. Y. City. A brilliant and
faithful student, and a very successful Private Teacher of French
at Burlington, Vt. He was a member of the First Baptist Church
of Burlington, Vt., for some years, but united with the Burlington First Congregational (Unitarian) Society in 1903, and is a
good helper there. Is a sturdy Republican. A member of Washington Lodge, No. 3, Free and Accepted Masons.

(8) JOHN EDWIN HIGGINS b. Webster, Me., Oct. 30, 1850;
resides on a farm at Danvers, Mass.; for several years he was a
very successful business man at Peabody, Mass.; he then had
blood poisoning in a severe form, and since then his health has
been much impaired; he is highly respected at home and abroad
as an upright and true-hearted man. M. Dec. 7, 1893, Lauretta
May Stevens of Peabody, Mass.; a woman of noble and helpful
character.

(9) LLOYD STEVENS HIGGINS b. June 28, 1901.

(8) CORDELIA HIGGINS b. Lisbon, Me., June 28, 1860;
address, Bowdoinham, Me., R. F. D. No. 3, Box 83; graduated
from the Marr School, Lisbon, Me. For many years she has been
an excellent member of the West Bowdoin, Me., Free Baptist
Church, and is a woman very faithful in every duty of life, having
inherited in large degree the noble qualities of both her parents.
M. June 27, 1883, James Everett Wagg, b. Auburn, Me., Oct. 8,
1859; an honest, faithful and temperate man, with a good standing in every community where he has lived. Studied in the
Auburn, Me., schools; has been a very thorough workman in
various shoe manufactories until he moved to the large farm
where he now resides. He is the son of James Wagg of
Auburn, Me., who for several terms was Republican Representative to the Maine Legislature.

(9) JOHN EVERETT WAGG b. Aug. 10, 1885; d. Danvers,

Mass., Jan. 11, 1907 (21-6) ; a very honest and promising young man; a successful traveling salesman; m. Feb. 6, 1906, Mary Elizabeth Young b. Salem, Mass., Aug. 5, 1886. No children.

(9) JAMES WAGG b. Auburn, Me., Aug. 27, 1889; of great help to his father on the home farm, and of great cheer to both parents; he graduated from the Dingley High School, Lisbon Falls, Me.

(9) ALICE LINWOOD WAGG b. Auburn, Me., July 20, 1891 ; graduated from Dingley Grammar School, Lisbon Falls, Me.; and made fine records in the three years' time of study in the Lisbon Falls, Me., High School; a very efficient helper at home; a young woman of pure and noble character. M. Dec. 25, 1909, Benjamin Franklin Jones b. in the Mining Settlement of Muggsville, California, Apr. 22, 1874; has been a very efficient worker in many towns East and West; travelling salesman; now employed by Joseph Elwell and Company of Auburn, Me., as a broker. A faithful attendant with his wife at the West Bowdoin, Me., Free Baptist Church. The son of Nathan John Jones, b. Jamestown, Clay County, Missouri, and d. June 17, 1892; a miner and rancher; and of Phœbe Ann Jones b. Aug. 8, 1830, d. Apr. 16, 1898; she was descended from a strong old Welch family.

(9) ELLA WAGG b. Lisbon, Me., Oct. 21, 1893; a fine scholar, and a thoughtful helper of her parents.

(9) WILLIAM WAGG b. Lisbon, Me., May 2, 1896; studied in schools of Lisbon Falls and Bowdoin, Me.; a sturdy and cheery helper on the farm.

(9) LENA J. WAGG b. Dec. 4, 1904 ;d. Aug. 20, 1906; "a dear little blind girl, with a bright and intellectual face."

CHAPTER TWO

THE RECORDS OF WILDER PERRY (6)

* * *

(6) WILDER PERRY, the fourth child of Captain John Perry and Lucy Wooster, b. East Thomaston, now Rockland, Me., March 29, 1781; d. at Northport, Me., March 11, 1850. He resided at North Haven, Me., until 1830, when he removed to Northport, Me., where he was a very successful farmer, and a man of great uprightness and helpfulness of character. He and his wife were very devoted to their family, and both were faithful members of the Baptist Church. M. Nov. 27, 1817, Hannah Young b. Truro, Mass., Aug. 19, 1794; d. Lincolnville, Me., Sept. 16, 1875. She was a woman of great nobility of character, and descended from one of the strong old Massachusetts families. Sketch of her family kindly furnished by Mrs. Angelia F. French, Lincolnville, Me.: "My great-grandfather, Samuel Young, was buried at Orleans, Mass. My grandfather, Samuel Young, was born in 1755 and died at Vinalhaven, Me., in 1819; m. Lydia Stutt who was born on Cape Cod, Mass., and had relatives at Truro and Wellfleet, Mass. The following is list of the children of my grandfather, Samuel Young, though they may not be arranged in their proper order. Samuel Young, Jr., lived to a good old age at Vinalhaven, Me.; m. Lydia ———. Mary Young m. Sylvanus Coombs and lived and died in Camden, Me. The members of this family are all dead so far as I know—Lydia Young m. Phineas Philbrook, and he and his family lived at Vinalhaven, Me.—Her twin sister, Rebecca Young, m. Mr. Dyer and lived in Vinalhaven, Me.—Martha Young m. Rev. Ezekiel Philbrook and lived at Freeport, Me., where they had a large family.—Hannah Young m. Wilder Perry.—David Young m. lived and died at Vinalhaven, Me. The first children of Wilder Perry were born at North Haven, Me., the last two were born Northport, Me."

* * *

(7) JAMES PERRY b. June 21, 1819; d. Feb. 19, 1891. In his early life he kept a country store at Lincolnville Beach, Me. He

served as Postmaster when Mr. Polk was President. He removed to Camden, Me., on the last day of 1856, and kept a store there until he retired from business. He served one term as Representative in the Maine Legislature, and was a very efficient Town Treasurer for several years. He and his wife were very faithful members of the Baptist Church. M. Aug. 12, 1844, Mrs. Sybil (Sherman) Pendleton, b. Islesboro, Me., Sept. 25, 1818, and died Nov. 22, 1902, at the age of 84 years. She m. (1st) Peleg Pendleton. She was the daughter of James Sherman and Sybil Gilkey; granddaughter of Robert Sherman and Eunice Turner; the only child of her first marriage died in infancy.

(8) CORA ISABEL PERRY b. Apr. 18, 1845; resides 157 Atlantic Ave., Providence, R. I.; m. (1st) Aug. 16, 1867, Dr. Edward T. Fuller, a very successful physician at Sedgwick and Camden, Me.; d. at Camden, Me. M. (2d) June 6, 1877, Nicholas Luther Berry b. at Camden, Me. Child of first marriage:

(9) GRACE CLIFF BERRY b. Feb. 3, 1878; resides Lenox St., Providence, R. I.; m. John R. Bemis.

(10) Sybil Hope Bemis.

(10) Son b. Feb. 5, 1911.

(8) JAMES OSMOND PERRY b. Nov. 12, 1846; d. July 8, 1872.

(8) WILDER WASHINGTON PERRY b. Nov. 24, 1848; resides Camden, Me.; for many years has been a traveling salesman for Houghton, Mifflin & Co., Boston, Mass. Graduated at Colby University, 1872. In 1893 he attended, as the Honorable Representative from Maine, the World's Fair at Vienna, and has traveled extensively in America and Europe. From 1874 to 1883 he was editor and publisher of the Camden, Me., Herald, and was its publisher until 1891. He was then a real estate and insurance agent at Camden, Me. 1892-1893 he was editor of the Portland, Me., Prohibition Herald, and Chairman of the State Prohibition Committee. He twice served very efficiently in the Maine Legislature, 1878 and 1879, and in the spring of 1879 and 1880 was representative of the Greenback Party. He is a man of untiring energy, and of sterling qualities, and has always been deeply interested in educational and political matters. M. Oct. 31, 1876, Mary Belle Ladd Sherman b. Camden, Me., May 9, 1853; a very fine student at St. Mary's Hall, Burlington, N. J.; the daughter of Ignatius Sherman of Camden, Me., and of Elithea Graffam of East Thomaston, now Rockland, Me. Mr.

Perry and his wife are very helpful members of the Baptist Church. Their children born Camden, Me.

(9) DR. SHERMAN PERRY b. June 11, 1878; Head Surgeon of the Children's Hospital, Boston, Mass.; graduated from Colby College, 1901; a very successful teacher at Morristown, N. J., for two years; graduated from Harvard Medical College, 1907; served for eighteen months as House Officer of the City Hospital, Worcester, Mass.; a very successful physician and surgeon.

(9) HOWARD PERRY b. June 9, 1879; d. Jan. 29, 1903 (23); graduated from Vermont Academy, Saxton's River, Vt.; at the time of his death he was studying in his second year in the University of Dentistry, Philadelphia, Pa. A young man of great ability and promise.

(9) FLORENCE PERRY b. July 8, 1881; resides Friendship, Me.; graduated from Coburn Classical Institute, and studied two years in Colby College; a fine teacher at Camden, Me.; a faithful member of the Baptist Church; resided Camden, Me., 1881-1890; in Portland, Me., 1890-1891; Camden, Me., until 1907; since then in Friendship, Me. M. Apr. 8, 1907, Dr. William Harding Hahn of Friendship, Me., b. Rockland, Me., Oct. 27, 1878; graduated from Vermont Academy, 1899; from Baltimore, Md., Medical College, 1904; a good physician; Knight of Pythias; the son of Myron Jacob Hahn and Flora Webber of Rockland, Me.

(9) DAVID PERRY b. Mch. 8, 1883; d. Jan. 23, 1897.

(9) PAUL PERRY b. July 19, 1884; d. Dec. 8, 1886.

(9) MILDRED PERRY b. July 30, 1886; a teacher in Art in Wesleyan Academy, Wilbraham, Mass.; graduated from the Normal Art School, Boston, Mass., 1907.

(9) JAMES PERRY b. May 17, 1888; a fine student in Colby College.

(9) GEORGE WATERHOUSE PERRY b. Sept. 19, 1891.

(9) JONAS GLEASON PERRY b. May 7, 1894.

(8) LEILA TRANTINE PERRY b. June 30, 1851; resides 3 Marine Ave., Camden, Me.; has resided in Camden, Waterville and Portland, Me.; graduated from Camden, Me., High School, and studied one year in Coburn Classical Institute, Waterville, Me. A faithful member of the Camden Baptist Church. M. (1st) Nov. 24, 1874, Frank A. Champlin of Waterville, Me.; b. Sept. 13, 1849, the son of James T. Champlin, D.D., LL.D., and of Mary Ann Pierce of Providence, R. I.; these parents resided

in Waterville and Portland, Me. M. (2d) Oct. 22, 1889 Willis
Williams b. Northport, Me., Mch. 11, 1855; yacht builder and
sailing master; a very worthy citizen; the son of David Williams
and Orinda Philbrook. Child of the first marriage:

(9) ALMIRA PIERCE CHAMPLIN b. July 15, 1878; d. Aug.
30, 1882.

Child of the second marriage:

(9) EDWARD D. WILLIAMS b. Oct. 20, 1891; d. May 29, 1893.

(8) FRANK WINSLOW PERRY b. Lincolnville, Me., Feb. 20,
1854; resides Lincolnville, Me.; R. F. D.; has lived Camden, Me.,
1857-1878; Boston, Mass., 1878-1880; Camden, Me., 1880-1890;
Somerville, Mass., 1890-1909; graduated from Camden, Me.,
graded schools, 1872; from a Private School, 1873; from a Business School, 1874; a dry goods merchant and salesman; member
of the Dry Goods Clerks' Benefit Association of Boston, Mass.;
m. Apr. 10, 1884, Lila Babcock Adams, Lincolnville, Me., June
10, 1861; graduated from Lincolnville, Me., schools and schools
of Boston, Mass., in 1874; the daughter of Charles Thompson
Adams and Elizabeth Ann Smart who lived in Charlestown,
Mass., and in Swanville, Me. She is thus a direct descendant of
the celebrated John Adams Family and of Major Joseph Smart.

(9) CHARLES ADAMS PERRY b. Camden, Me., Mch. 10, 1886;
resides Auburn, Me.; resided Camden, Me., until 1890; in
Somerville, Mass., until 1908; Concord, N. H., 1908-1909; in
Manchester, N. H., until 1910; since then at Auburn, Me.; graduated from Edgerly Grammar School, Somerville, Mass., 1900;
from Somerville English High School, 1904; from Mass. Normal
Art School, 1908. While a student at the Mass. Art School he
was President of his Class in his Junior and Senior years, and
Secretary of his Class in his Freshman year; he was one of the
very efficient editors of the Art School paper, The Center of
Vision. At the time of his graduation he was selected by the
Faculty of the Art School to represent his course, that of Con-
structive Arts. 1908-1910; served as a member of the Board of
Directors of the Mass. Normal Art School Alumni Association
During his senior year he was connected with P. A. Fisher, the
Boston Architect, thus working upon many fine City residences.
While a student he was Vice President of the School Glee Club
and a member of the Varsity Baseball and Basketball Teams. He
has been the designer and builder of a gasoline marine engine
which bears the name "Perry," and has also designed and built

CHARLES ADAMS PERRY

several motor boats. Assistant Librarian Somerville, Mass., Public Library, 1901-1907; Assistant Curator of Mass. Normal Art School, 1907. Instructor in Concord, N. H., Mechanic Arts, High School, 1908-1909; Master in Manchester, N. H., Manual Training School, 1909-1910. Since then Department of Manual Training, Auburn, Me. A faithful member of the Baptist Church. Member of King David's Lodge F. & A. M., Lincolnville, Me. A brilliant and trustworthy young man.

(8) ANNIE PORTER PERRY b. Lincolnville, Me., June 7, 1856; resides Saco, Me.; resided Camden, Me., until Feb., 1881; in Saco, Me., since then; graduated from Camden, Me., High School, 1873; taught school one year; graduated from Coburn Classical Institute, June, 1876; a very helpful member of the Baptist Church in the Maine towns, Camden, Waterville, and Saco. Attended the International Christian Endeavor Convention, N. Y. City, 1892; and in Boston, Mass., 1895; attended the Baptist National Anniversaries in Washington, D. C., May, 1907; member of the Daughters of the American Revolution; has attended many Annual Meetings of the Maine Federation of Women's Clubs. M. Feb. 15, 1881, Burton Hockey Winslow b. Freedom, Me., Jan. 21, 1855; graduated from Lewiston, Me., High School, 1871; was Draughtsman in an Architect's Office; Paymaster at the Cotton Mills of the Pepperell Manufacturing Co., Biddeford, Me.; has been the very successful publisher of Sunday School Concert Exercises since 1887; editor of monthly religious papers, 1878-1879; for nearly twenty-four years Deacon in the Baptist Church, having been a very efficient member of the Baptist Churches of Chelsea, Mass., and in Lewiston and Saco, Me. He has been Sunday School Superintendent for fourteen years, and has held many Church, State, and local offices. The son of Deacon Allen Pilsbury Winslow and of Lonathy Adeline Hockey, these parents having lived in Waterville and Saco, Me. The children born in Saco, Me., all of sterling character.

(9) EDWARD BURTON WINSLOW b. Dec. 16, 1881; resides 31 W. 61st St., N. Y. City; having gone there in the autumn of 1904. Graduated from Thornton Academy, Saco, Me., 1900; from Colby College, 1904. While a student at Thornton Academy was manager of a school monthly publication; at Colby College served in the Glee Club for four years; Orchestra for four years; on the Dramatic Club three years, being its President in his Senior year. One of the editors of the *Colby Echo* for four years, and

was its manager in his Senior year. Member of the Class and College Track team. Class Treasurer in his Junior and Senior years. Delta Kappa Epsilon delegate to National Convention in Washington, D. C., 1902; teacher of cheering at athletic games, hence his nickname, "Windy." A constant attendant at the Calvary Baptist Church, N. Y. City; having a perfect record of attendance in the Calvary Choir of 125 voices. Member of Delta Kappa Epsilon and of N. Y. City Alumni Association of Delta Kappa Epsilon. Employed by the Winthrop Press, N. Y. City, for over five years, learning every department of the printing business; 421 Lafayette St., N. Y. City. He got acquainted with Mr. John A. Eggers, President of the Winthrop Press, by shining his shoes at a summer hotel; entered his employ 1904; started by tying up bundles; spent three years learning the business; excellent salesman. Apr. 1, 1911, became purchasing Agent for the Am. So. of Mechanical Engineers, 29 W. 29th St., N. Y. M. Apr. 19, 1911, Gertrude Koelsch, a fine young lady and member of Calvary Baptist Church, N. Y. City.

(9) NELLIE PERRY WINSLOW b. Apr. 12, 1884; resides 35 Thornton Ave., Saco, Me.; graduated from Thornton Academy, Saco, Me.; 1902; graduated from Colby College, 1907; member of the Baptist Church.

(9) ARTHUR KENELM WINSLOW b. Oct. 29, 1885; Instructor in Greek, Latin and History, Higgins Institute, Charleston, Me.; graduated from Thornton Academy, Saco, Me., 1903; from Colby College, 1907; in 1908 worked in the Circulation Department of Scribner's Magazine, N. Y. City; member of the Baptist Church.

(9) CLARA ELIOT WINSLOW b. May 4, 1891; graduated from Thornton Academy, Saco, Me., 1909; entered Colby College, 1909; member of the Baptist Church.

(9) WINTHROP WINSLOW b. Jan. 25, 1893; studied in Thornton Academy, Saco, Me., three years; left there 1909 to complete his College preparatory course in Higgins Classical Institute, Charleston, Me., and entered Colby College, Sept., 1910; member of Baptist Church.

(8) NELLIE SOPHIA PERRY b. Oct. 4, 1858; resides 271 Crafts St., Newtonville, Mass.; m. Dec. 6, 1882, John Richard Prescott of Newtonville, Mass.

(9) HELEN WINSLOW PRESCOTT b. Jan. 15, 1888.

(9) MARION ISABEL PRESCOTT b. Mch. 9, 1890.

(9) RICHARD MACEY PRESCOTT b. Jan. 29, 1893; d. Dec. 3, 1895.

(8) GRACE DARLING PERRY b. Camden, Me., June 19, 1861; resides Bard Hall, Military Academy, Cornwall-on-the-Hudson; has lived in towns of Maine, Rhode Island, Conn., N. Y., Ill., and California; graduated from Camden, Me., High School; Providence, R. I., High School; studied music in Providence, R. I.; carefully managed a family estate for seven years; faithful member of the Baptist Church, m. June 21, 1898, Major Edward H. Baker, b. Camden, Me., July 11, 1862. Educated in Chicago, Ill., N. Y. City, and in private study; Commandant and Superintendent of Military Academies; served and commissioned in Illinois National Guards 1879-1885; commissioned again 1889; commissioned in National Guard of Missouri, 1899; the son of Charles H. Baker, who resided in Norridgewock and Skowhegan, Me., Springfield, Mass., Washington, D. C.; resided in California, 1853-1856; since 1867 has resided in Chicago, Ill. He married Emily A. Cobb, who resided in Camden, Me., and in Holliston, Mass., until her marriage.

* * *

(7) JANE PERRY, the second child of Wilder Perry, b. Sept. 25, 1820, d. Apr. 23, 1903; a noble and helpful woman; in her last illness her eldest son cared for her in a very faithful manner; she resided for many years at Lincolnville, Me.; m. Aug. 10, 1840, Capt. Elbridge Drinkwater of Northport, Me., b. Feb. 5, 1811, d. June 1, 1868; a very successful sea Captain, and a worthy citizen. Children born at Lincolnville, Me.

(8) CELESTE JANE DRINKWATER b. May 23, 1841; d. June 12, 1859.

(8) EMILY HORTENSE DRINKWATER b. Jan. 29, 1843; resides Lincolnville, Me.; m. May 31, 1867, Capt. John H. Monroe, a very efficient commander of vessels.

(9) MARION CELESTE MONROE b. Apr. 14, 1868; m. Mch. 4, 1901, A. Lincoln Raymond of Boston.

(9) J. ALTON MONROE b. Aug. 1, 1874; mariner residing at Northport, Me.; m. Sept. 24, 1898, Lida M. Peckard b. Aug. 31, 1879.

(8) CAPT. MARION ELBRIDGE DRINKWATER b. Nov. 23, 1846; unmarried.

(8) CAPT. WILDER PERRY DRINKWATER b. Mch. 15, 1851; resides Lincolnville, Me.; a very successful sea Captain for fifteen

years; then a farmer; Free Mason; m. Dec. 5, 1873, Imogene
Julia Thomas b. Sept. 26, 1851, d. Dec. 28, 1899, the daughter of
Chandler O. Thomas and Mary E. Coombs of Lincolnville, Me.
Children b. Lincolnville, Me.

(9) ISABEL JANE DRINKWATER b. Mch. 19, 1875, d. Aug. 11,
1905; m. Jan. 14, 1899, Frank M. Brown b. May 19, 1875; seaman; no children.

(9) GILBERT THOMAS DRINKWATER b. June 1, 1877; a
farmer at Lakeside, San Diego County, California; studied in
Lincolnville, Me., schools; has also been employed in sawmills
and in railroad work; to Boston, Mass., 1899; in Seattle, Washington, 1900-1902; San Francisco, Calif., 1903-1907; in Lakeside,
Calif., since then; m. June 5, 1899, Jessica L. Clay b. Rockland,
Me., June 15, 1879; graduated from Montpelier, Vt., High
School; the daughter of Orrin E. Clay and Leonia Hendricks,
who resided at Blue Hill, Me., and at Montpelier, Vt.

(9) ARTHUR D. DRINKWATER b. Mch. 11, 1879, d. Mch. 6,
1897.

(9) ALLYNE PERRY DRINKWATER b. Sept. 29, 1885; m. Apr.
22, 1905, Robie Frank Ames b. June 22, 1885.

(10) ISABEL ZILPHA AMES b. Feb. 5, 1906.

(10) MERTON HOWARD AMES b. Mch. 3, 1907.

(9) ALICE EMILY DRINKWATER b. Sept. 5, 1886; m. Nov. 23,
1908, Milbury Hunt.

(9) ANGIE MONROE DRINKWATER b. Nov. 21, 1887.

(9) JESSIE W. DRINKWATER b. Oct. 16, 1891.

(9) MARION ELBRIDGE DRINKWATER b. Oct. 16, 1891.

(8) CHARLES J. DRINKWATER b. Jan. 13, 1854; resides Camden, Me.; m. Nov. 29, 1874, Cora Livingstone Monroe.

(9) EDNA WITHINGTON DRINKWATER b. Feb. 18, 1877; d.
Sept. 25, 1897.

(9) WILLIAM ELBRIDGE DRINKWATER b. Oct. 23, 1878.

(9) ELMER BATES DRINKWATER b. Oct. 8, 1879.

(9) SARAH THOMPSON DRINKWATER b. Nov. 27, 1883.

(9) EMILY HORTENSE DRINKWATER b. July 16, 1891; d. Oct.
9, 1891.

(9) MYRON CHARLES DRINKWATER b. Oct. 21, 1895.

* * *

(7) REV. DAVID PERRY b. Apr. 14, 1822; d. at Boston, Mass.,
May 27, 1859. He received a fine education, and was a very suc-

cessful teacher at Owl's Head, Me.; and then taught Navigation in his home. He was a very faithful minister, and was beloved by many people; he was first settled in the ministry at Camden, Me., where he was ordained in 1850. He also preached with rare helpfulness at Union and South Thomaston, Me. One who knew him well wrote in a leading newspaper, "He distinguished himself by a blameless life and an untiring assiduity in his profession. He died suddenly from erysipelas. His last words were spoken with great calmness, 'Yes, the Lord doeth all things well.' He was buried with Masonic honors at Camden, Me. Rev. Dr. Kalloch said in his funeral sermon, 'He was a rare man, sincere, true, manly and firm in all relations, duties and offices of life. He has left a character without a stain, and a memory which is a priceless legacy.' He was a kind husband and father, and esteemed by all parties and creeds as a discreet and useful minister. He took a deep interest in education, and in moral reform. He was a noble Pastor." M. May 2, 1846, Jane Patience Rogers, b. Jan. 13, 1825; resides 103 Williams St., Chelsea, Mass.; she is remakably preserved for one of her age. She graduated at a Select School at Bangor, Me., and was a very successful teacher before her marriage. She has ever been a woman of noble and helpful character. She was the daughter of Captain Atherton Wales Rogers, who is said to have been born at Castine, Me., Nov. 13, 1793; resided at Lincolnville, Me., and was lost at sea 1845; m. July 1822, Celia Rogers, the daughter of Adam Rogers and Rachel Wales; she d. June 22, 1831; and her husband m. (2) in 1833 Susan Mariner Miller; of their six children the only survivor is George Atherton Rogers of S. Weymouth, Mass. The only sister of Jane Patience Rogers was Rachel Wales Rogers, who died in infancy.

(8 DAVID ATHERTON PERRY d. in infancy.

(8) ACHSAH EMERETTA PERRY d. in infancy.

(8) CELIA HANNAH PERRY b. Lincolnville, Me., Dec. 25, 1848; has resided at 103 Williams St., Chelsea, Mass., for many years. Early in life she learned the custom vest making trade, in which she has had fine success. She is a noble, helpful daughter and friend. Unm.

* * *

(7) JOHN CHARLES PERRY b. Sept. 30, 1824, lost on Trundy's Reef, near Portland, Me., Dec. 6, 1869; Captain sailing to coastwise ports; m. May 1, 1856, Alice Irene Matthews, b. Lincoln-

ville, Me., Dec. 21, 1839; resides 2 Grove St., Belfast, Me.; her
parents reside at Lincolnville, Me.

(8) JOHN CHARLES WILTONPERRY b. Lincolnville, Me., July 3,
1858; resides 74 Winter St., Portland, Me.; has also lived Bel-
fast, Me., Minneapolis, Minn., Peoria, Ill., etc. Graduated from
Belfast, Me., High School 1877; Free Mason; Knight of
Pythias; member of United Commercial Travelers; commercial
traveler; m. Sept. 3 1890, Charlotte Mary Ricker, b. Portland,
Me., July 10, 1865; graduated from Portland, Me., High School,
1883; daughter of Horace Hannibal Ricker and Susan Maria
Chapman, these parents residing in the Maine towns, Paris,
Poland and Portland, Me.

(9) HORACE RICKER PERRY b. Peoria, Ill., Dec. 3, 1894;
graduated from Butler Grammar School, Portland, Maine, June,
1910.

(9) ALICE MATTHEWS PERRY b. Portland, Me., Mch. 18,
1896; graduated from Butler Grammar School, Portland, Me.,
June, 1910.

(8) RALPH MILLER PERRY b. Lincolnville, Me., Feb. 19,
1865, d. at 2 Grove Street, Belfast, Me., Feb. 4, 1910; from
tuberculosis; studied in Lincolnville, Me., schools, and graduated
from Gray's Business College; attended the Unitarian Church; a
very successful Hotel Manager; m. Aug. 23, 1901, Elizabeth
Havener Patch, b. East Northport, Me., Jan. 11, 1878; studied in
Northport, Me., schools; the daughter of George Herbert Patch
and Orilla Belle Cross; no children.

* * *

(7) GEORGE PERRY b. May 14, 1826; d. May 25, 1826.

* * *

(7) RACHEL W. PERRY b. Oct. 29, 1828; d. at Lincolnville,
Me., Sunday morning, Jan. 17, 1904 (75). "Fifty-two years ago
Rachel Perry was united in marriage to Captain Israel S. Adams,
and during all these years she was a true and loyal companion.
No wife was ever more helpful to her husband. Safe in counsel,
the heart of her husband fully trusted in her. Many were the
duties and responsibilities which rested upon her during her husband's absences from home, for, for many years, he was one of
the best-known sea Captains of Maine. Her life was full of
cheerfulness and brightness, carrying to those about her joy and

comfort, and especially to the members of her own home. It was here that her Christian life shed forth rays of sunshine amid the perplexities and discouragements of life. Home was her empire, and love its throne, and nothing which she could do to increase the happiness of those committed to her care was left undone. But while her death caused great sorrow to her family, they can rejoice in the Christian influence which she leaves behind her as an inspiration to them to live the life of faith in the Son of God. One of the pillars of the community in which she lived has been removed that it might be placed in the temple not made with hands eternal in the heavens. In this hour of sorrow the sympathy of the entire community goes out to this bereaved family who mourn their loss. Early on Sunday morning she quietly and beautifully as the unfolding of the rose slipped away to the King in His beauty, and to receive a crown of righteousness from His hand. Her kindness and sympathy with every one with whom she came in contact bound her with cords of love to many in the community. Rev. L. D. Evans of Camden, Me., conducted the funeral services. Rachel W. Perry m. Aug. 18, 1851, Capt. Israel S. Adams, b. Lincolnville, Me., Nov. 4, 1825. The *Boston Sunday Globe* for December, 1909, says, "Capt. Israel S. Adams, formerly of the Florence Leland, recently passed his 84th birthday at the home of his daughter, Mrs. Roscoe McKeen, 11 Copeland St., Roxbury, Mass. He takes long walks and reads the news of the day. He spends his summers down on his farm at Lincolnville, Me., where he has a small garden. He ploughs and plants and raises all the vegetables used on the home table. Speaking of his rugged health, Capt. Adams says, 'Sick? I should say not. Why, when I first went to sea—I was only a boy of twelve—my Uncle said, No, you'd better stay at home; you'll be seasick. But I went, and I wasn't seasick. And I haven't been sick since. Most of my trips were from New York to the West Indies with general cargoes. I've been in every kind of a storm, but was never wrecked. The quickest and pleasantest voyage that I ever made was from New York to the Canary Islands, then to Brunswick, and back to New York. We made that in two months. The weather was perfect and all the crew in fine condition. You don't often get a long trip like that when everything goes well.' Capt. Adams don't mind wintering in town as long as he can go down East in May and keep in touch with his former business, as well as enjoy his work as a gardener."

Children of Rachel W. Perry and Capt. Israel S. Adams:

(8) HANNAH PERRY ADAMS b. June 18, 1855; resides Culbertson, Nebraska; m. in Roxbury, Mass., Nov. 23, 1904, Rev. Hiram E. McFarlane, who is now Pastor of the Methodist Episcopal Church at Culbertson, Neb.; where he and his wife are greatly beloved for their faithful services.

(8) FANNIE CELESTE ADAMS b. Sept. 26, 1859; resides Freeport, Me.; m. Nov. 16, 1887, Jarvis Adelbert Brewster, who is the successful Proprietor of a Grocery Store; they are very helpful citizens.

(9) MABEL CARRIE BREWSTER b. Mch. 4, 1889; d. Feb. 19, 1896.

(8) NETTIE LULA ADAMS b. Sept. 2, 1864; resides 11 Copeland St., Roxbury, Mass.; a woman of great cheer and helpfulness; graduated from Castine, Me., Normal School, 1883; m. Dec. 1, 1891, Roscoe De Witte McKeen, b. Swanville, Me., Jan. 8, 1866; graduated from Castine, Me., Normal School, 1884; he has been the very successful Superintendent of Schools, at East Bridgewater, Mass., and at Haverhill, Mass.; on account of ill health he gave up this work for several years; and bought the business at 146 Dudley St., Roxbury, Mass.; the son of Ephraim McKeen and Sarah Jane Nickerson who resided at Swanville and Belfast, Me.

(8) CARRIE EDNA ADAMS b. Apr. 13, 1869; resides 11 Copeland St., Roxbury, Mass.; graduated from Haverhill, Mass., Commercial College; for several years a very efficient stenographer in Boston, Mass.

* * *

(7) CAPT. EPHRAIM PERRY b. Apr. 29, 1830; has resided at Hallowell, Me., for many years, where he is a highly-esteemed citizen; followed the sea for forty-five years, for most of the time being a Captain who was widely known for his wide-awake and enterprising character. He retired from the sea in Nov., 1889; resided Lincolnville, Me., from 1851 to 1869; from then until Nov., 1890, lived in Camden, Me.; m. Feb. 3, 1856, Mary F. Knight, b. Lincolnville, Me., Mch. 12, 1836, a very kind and helpful woman; the daughter of Nathan Knight and Lucy Dean. Children b. Lincolnville Me.

(8) WALLACE HENRY PERRY b. Feb. 3, 1859; has been a very worthy citizen of Hallowell, Me., for over twenty-two years; Cashier of the Hallowell, Me., National Bank for twenty years;

graduated from Maine Wesleyan Seminary, Kent's Hill, Me., in 1884; he and his wife are excellent members of the Methodist Episcopal Church; m. Sept. 15, 1890, Harriet E. McClench, b. Hallowell, Me., Jan. 3, 1859; the daughter of George B. McClench and Martha Gibbs Rose of Hallowell, Me.

(9) HARRIET LOUISE PERRY b. Sept. 15, 1891; graduated at Hallowell, Me., High School, 1909; has studied elocution in Augusta, Me.

(9) DONALD BURKE PERRY b. Oct. 26, 1896; studied in Hallowell, Me., schools.

(8) AUSTIN KNIGHT PERRY b. Oct. 3, 1863; resides Shiloh, Me.; resided at Lincolnville, Me., until 1869; at Camden, Me., until 1879; Auburn, Me., 1884 and 1885; Hallowell, Me., 1886 and 1887; Abilene, Kansas, 1887-1892; Tescott, Kansas, 1893 and 1894; Kansas City, Mo., 1894-1896; Shiloh, Me., 1897-1898; Chicago, Ill., 1899; Liverpool, England, 1900; Boston, Mass., 1901; Liverpool, England, 1902; Shiloh, Me., 1902-1909; in England as Commodore of the Kingdom Yacht Club a Gospel Fleet; graduated from Dirigo Business College, 1880; a printer 1884 and 1885; Cashier of Hallowell, Me., National Bank, 1886-1887; Assistant Bank Cashier, Abilene, Kansas, 1887-1888; Cashier of Bank, Abilene, Kansas, 1890-1892; ordained as an undenominational minister 1896; has preached in Kansas City, Mo.; Auburn, Me.; Chicago, Ill.; Liverpool, England; Boston, Mass., and in other places with great efficiency; in 1909 went to Palestine as Master of Bark Kingdom; m. Sept. 15, 1884, Hanna Arvilla Philbrook, b. Islesboro, Me., June 13, 1856; the daughter of Jabez Philbrook and Eliza J. McKenney.

(8) FRANK D. PERRY b. Sept. 4, 1865; d. June 6, 1871.

* * *

(7) CAPT. ROBERT W. PERRY b. June 9, 1832; has resided at Lincolnville, Me., for some years; he and his wife are highly esteemed; sea Captain for some time; then a merchant; Post Master for eight years; m. Jan. 18, 1857, Eliza Jane French, b. Jan. 16, 1839; the daughter of Eben French and Eliza Drinkwater who resided in Lincolnville and Northport, Me.

* * *

(7) ANGELIA FURBUSH PERRY b. Northport, Me., Jan. 23, 1836; has long resided at Lincolnville, Me., a woman of noblest character and of great helpfulness; studied in the schools of Lin-

colnville and Belfast, Me., and Waltham, Mass.; m. Sept. 6, 1856,
Captain Oscar Wyman French b. Lincolnville, Me., Dec. 21,
1834; studied in the Lincolnville, Me., schools; a very successful
Captain from 1858-1894, sailing to U. S. Ports from Eastport,
Me., to Florida; also to ports in the West Indies, Mexico and
South America; this family resided at Lincolnville, Me., until
1875; at Belfast, Me., 1875-1895; then returned to Lincolnville.
Capt. French is the son of Abel French b. Apr. 23, 1808; d. Apr.
21, 1889; resided Lincolnville, Me.; m. July 10, 1832, Jane
Drinkwater b. Dec. 24, 1810; d. Feb. 24, 1884; grandson of Heze-
kiah French and Eunice Rogers.

(8) JANE ISABEL FRENCH b. Oct. 6, 1859; resides 409 West
Fifth St., Reno, Nevada; has lived at Berkley, and in other California towns; a woman of superior qualities; m. Apr. 5, 1883,
Fred N. Fletcher b. China, Me., Sept. 15, 1856; graduated from
Colby University; a successful teacher for several years; then
editor of the *Pioneer,* Alpena, Mich.; has for several years been
deeply interested in mining; is now a very efficient mining engineer; for some time was Superintendent of King Solomon's
Mines, Siskiyou, California; he took a special course of study in
mining at Deer Lodge, Montana.

(9) ROBERT FRENCH FLETCHER b. Belfast, Me., Feb. 12,
1884; d. Jan. 25, 1885.

(9) ETHEL LOUISE FLETCHER b. Alpena, Mich., Jan. 22,
1886; a fine student in the Berkley, California, schools; in the
University of California, etc; a teacher at Reno, Nevada.

(9) HAROLD AUGUSTUS FLETCHER b. Dec. 10, 1888; Berkley,
California, schools; now a student in the University of Nevada.

(9) HOWARD FRENCH FLETCHER b. Helena, Montana, Sept.
12, 1893; schools of Berkley, Calif., and of Reno, Nevada.

(9) RUSSELL FLETCHER b. Aug. 20, 1899; schools of Berkley,
Calif., and of Reno, Nevada.

(8) MARY PERRY FRENCH b. Lincolnville, Me., July 5, 1862;
resides Rockland, Me., R. F. D.; has resided Belfast, Me., Bridgewater and Manchester, Mass.; and at Batavia, N. Y., for some
years; to Rockland, Me., 1904; graduated from Belfast, Me., High
School, 1880; from Gorham, Me., Normal School, 1882; m. June
19, 1886, John Franklin Rich b. Hope, Me., Apr. 17, 1855; studied in Maine Wesleyan Seminary, Kent's Hill, Me.; Castine, Me.,
Normal School; East Maine Conference Seminary, Bucksport,
Me.; Colby University; graduated from Wesleyan University,

Middletown, Conn., 1881; he was the very efficient Principal of the High Schools of Belfast, Me., and of Bridgewater, Mass.; Superintendent of Manchester, Mass., schools; Professor of Mathematics and Latin in Chamberlain Institute, Randolph, N. Y.; has also been traveling salesman for Ginn & Co., publishers of College and school text-books; now owns two fine farms near Rockland, Me.; Selectman of Rockport, Me., 1908-1909; he is the son of John Gilkey Rich and Sarah Gay Daggett who resided at Hope and Belmont, Me. Mr. and Mrs. Rich are very helpful members of the Methodist Episcopal Church.

(9) PERRY FRANK RICH b. Belfast, Me., Feb. 19, 1887; a fine student in the High Schools of Batavia, N. Y., and of Rockland, Me.; Mount Hermon, Mass., School and in Burdette's Business College, Boston, Mass. A young man of fine promise.

(8) LEON HOWARD FRENCH b. Jan. 14, 1868; resides 53 Washington Square, New York City; Pharmacist and salesman; graduated from the N. Y. College of Pharmacy; now a very successful commercial traveler.

(8) ROBERT ALLEN FRENCH b. Mch. 28, 1871; 825 Market St., San Francisco, Cal.; 1910 a fine salesman and buyer for a Philadelphia, Pa., Shoe Company; at Helena, Montana, he was a boot and shoe salesman for a Bangor, Me., firm; he also resided in Waltham, Mass., for a while.

CHAPTER THREE.

THE RECORDS OF HANNAH PERRY (6).

* * *

(6) HANNAH PERRY b. Feb. 18, 1784; d. Oct. 11, 1867; m. Dec. 15, 1805, John Ames, b. Nov. 8, 1782, d. May 13, 1861 (78) ; farmer and fisherman; son of Mark Ames, who m. Priscilla Howland and Rebecca Cushberry. This family always resided at North Haven, Maine.

* * *

(7) DURA AMES b. May 7, 1806; d. Dec. 2, 1825.

* * *

(7) CAPTAIN JESSE AMES b. Feb. 4, 1808; d. Dec. 6, 1894 (1898?) in Northfield, Minn.; he moved to Minnesota soon after his marriage, and was a very succesful miller at Northfield, Minn.; m. Oct. 27, 1832, Martha Bradbury Tolman, b. May 8, 1813; daughter of Thomas Tolman and Lydia Ingraham.

(8) JOHN THOMAS AMES b. Feb. 15, 1834; resided Northfield, Minn.; moved to St. Paul, Minn., in Apr., 1857; in 1860 he moved to Rice County, Minn., and farmed there for three years; returned to Northfield in 1863; farming in company with his father and brother; also raised much fine stock. He has twice been Mayor of Northfield, and thrice has been sent to a National Convention to help nominate a President. For several years he has been President of the Minn. Dairy Association. M. in Boston, Mass., July 9, 1858, Ellen Maria Clough; b. Bluehill, Me., Feb. 9, 1833; daughter of Moses Parker Clough and Sallie Peters Dodge.

(9) MARTHA ELLEN AMES b. St. Paul, Minn., May 18, 1859; m. Charles Fremont Nickels, b. Cherryfield, Me., July 9, 1856; Deputy Treasurer of Hennepin County, Minn.; book-keeper, Northfield, Minn.

(10) ELLEN NICKELS b. Northfield, Minn., Feb. 16, 1880.

(10) FRANCES NICKELS b. Feb. 10, 1882.

(9) SARAH FRANCES AMES b. St. Paul, Minn., Mch. 17, 1861; m. in Minneapolis, Sept. 26, 1884, Edward Henry Loyhed,

a hardware merchant in Faribault, Minn. B. Faribault, Minn., Apr. 15, 1858; of Thomas H. Loyhed and Lois A. Hicks.

(10) JOHN HENRY LOYHED b. Faribault, Minn., July 24, 1885; d. Aug. 23, 1887.

(10) THOMAS HENRY LOYHED b. Faribault, Mch. 30, 1887.

(10 BENJAMIN HENRY LOYHED, born Faribault, July 4, 1888; died Seattle, June 28, 1889.

(10) LOIS DOROTHY LOYHED b. Minneapolis, Minn., Nov. 3, 1889.

(10) KATHERINE LOYHED b. Seattle, Washington, Mch. 31, 1892.

(10) DONALD AMES LOYHED, b. April 5, 1897.

(9) ALICE ADELBERT AMES b. Cameron City, Minn., Dec. 12, 1864; m. in Northfield, Minn., Dec. 12, 1887, Alden Taylor Hall, a druggist of St. Paul, Minn.; b. Conn. Mch. 18, 1859.

(10) MARGARET AMES HALL b. St. Paul, Minn., Oct. 12, 1889.

(10) CATHERINE AMES HALL b. St. Paul, Nov. 29, 1891.

(9) JOHN ADELBERT AMES b. Northfield, Minn., Feb. 3, 1869; m. Tacoma, Wash., May 21, 1890, Josephine Edwards of Tacoma, Washington, b. Helena, Montana, May, 1870; Printer, Seattle, Wash.

(10) JESSE EDWARDS AMES b. Helena, Montana, Jan. 30, 1892; is a newspaper printer and writer, Spokane, Wash.

(8) GEN. ADELBERT AMES b. Oct. 31, 1835; resides Lowell, Mass. The following is the Adjutant General's report of Maine for the years 1864 and 1865: "Brevet Major Gen. Adelbert Ames. In June, 1856, he entered the Military Academy at West Point and graduated the fifth in his class as a Lieutenant, May, 1861. Immediately upon graduating he was ordered to Washington, and assigned duty as an instructor of one of the New York Militia Regiments. In June, being ordered to Griffin's, West Point, Battery, he took part in the first Bull Run action, in which he was severely wounded, and in consequence restrained from active service. Upon his recovery in Sept., he was assigned to Battery A., one of the batteries of the artillery Brigade under command of Col. Hunt, U. S. Artillery, of which he was given command, Oct. 1st. In Mch., 1862, Captain Ames started for Richmond, Va., under Gen. McLellan, when, being stationed at Yorktown, he fulfilled the duties of an engineer officer upon some of the works, in addition to those pertaining to his rank as a bat-

tery commander. Besides taking part in comparatively unimportant affairs, his battery was engaged at Garnett's Farm, June 27th, and also at Malvern Hill, for active participation in which campaign Captain Ames was recommended for two brevets. In August, being commissioned Col. of the 20th Regt., Me., Volunteers, he left the Army of the Potomac at Fortress Monroe to take command of that Regiment, which was subsequently assigned to the 5th Corps, and therefore bore a part in the campaign which culminated in the battles of Antietam and Fredericksburg. As numerous cases of virulent disease existed in the Regiment at that time, its members did not participate in the Battle of Chancellorsville, May 3d. Col. Ames, however, having offered his services as a volunteer aid, served in that campaign under Gens. Meade and Hooker. He was then appointed as a Brigadier Gen. of Volunteers, on the 20th of May, and assigned to the command of the 1st Brigade, 2d Division, 11th Corps. Early in the month of June, in command of a picket Brigade, from the different Corps, Gen. Ames, in connection with our cavalry, was engaged in a fight at Beverly Ford, Va., our forces being under the command of Gen. Pleasonton. A few days afterwards he rejoined the 11th Corps and participated in the battle of Gettysburgh, when Gen. Barlow was the Division commander, being wounded, on the first day's fight, the command during the continuance of the battle to 3d of July devolved upon Gen. Ames. On the 6th of Aug. the General, with his command, left the Army of the Potomac to report at Morris Island, S. C., and was there present at the siege of Fort Sumpter."

Johnson's Cyclopedia: "Gen. Ames graduated at West Point, 1861; Lieutenant Colonel Twenty-fourth Infantry, July 28, 1866; and Brigadier-General U. S. Vols. May 20, 1863. Brevetted Major Gen. Mch. 13, 1865, for gallant and meritorious service in the field. After the War was made Provisional Governor of Mississippi, June 15, 1868, in command of the fourth military district, department of Miss., 1869; resigned Feb. 23, 1870; U. S. Senator from Miss., 1870-73; Governor of State of Miss. 1874-76."

Gen. Adelbert Ames m. July 21, 1870, Blanche Butler, b. Mch. 2, 1847; a noble and helpful wife and mother; graduated from the Academy of the Visitation, Georgetown, D. C.; the daughter of Gen. B. F. Butler and of Sarah Hildreth of Lowell, Mass.

(9) Col. Butler Ames b. Lowell, Mass., Aug. 22, 1871; educated in the schools of Lowell, Mass.; graduated from Phillips Exeter, N. H., Academy, 1890; graduated from the U. S. Military Academy, West Point, N. Y., 1894; resigned from the U. S. Army after being appointed to the Eleventh U. S. Infantry, for the purpose of taking a Post Graduate Course at the Mass. Institute of Technology; graduating there in 1896 as a mechanical and electrical engineer; afterwards was Agent for the Wamesit Power Company of Lowell, Mass.; joined Light Battery A., Mass. Volunteer Militia, a Sergeant at its re-organization in 1895; acted as its Instructor and was promoted to 1st Lieut. in 1896; resigned from the Militia at the outbreak of the Spanish American War, and was made a Lieutenant and then Adjutant of the Sixth Mass. Volunteers. At Camp Alger, near Washington, D. C., he was appointed Acting Engineer of the Second Army Corps, under Gen. Graham, in addition to his duties as Adjutant; went to Cuba and Porto Rico under Gen. Miles; was at the landing at Guanica, and at the skirmish at Yauco Road in July; promoted to Lt. Col. of his Regiment in August; Civil Administrator of Arecibo District of Porto Rico until Nov., 1898. He served as a member of the Common Council of Lowell, Mass., in 1896; a member of the Mass. Legislature for the three years, 1897, 1898, and 1899; Chairman of the Committee on Street Railways; elected to the Fifty-eighth, fifty-ninth and sixtieth Congresses; re-elected to the sixty-first Congress, receiving 16,-251 votes, to 11,910 for Joseph J. Flynn, Democrat, and 845 for George Conley of the Independent League."

(9) Edith Ames b. Mch. 4, 1873; R. F. D. No. 111, Lowell, 'Mass.; studied in Bryn Mawr College, Pa., 1891-'93; m. June 17, 1896, Charles Brooks Stevens b. Haverhill, Mass., Oct. 11, 1864; graduated from Harvard College, 1886; a woolen manufacturer at Lowell, Mass.; the son of George Stevens and Harriet Lyman Brooks of Newport, R. I.

(10) Ames Stevens b. May 31, 1897.

(10) Edith Stevens b. January 23, 1898.

(10) Harriet Lyman Stevens b. July 19, 1900.

(10) Brooks Stevens, Jr., b. Dec. 20, 1902.

(9) Sarah Hildreth Ames b. Oct. 1, 1874; graduated at Miss Baldwin's School, Bryn Mawr, Pa.; studied two years in Bryn Mawr College, Class of 1897; m. June 1, 1901, Spencer Borden, Jr., b. Fall River, Mass., Sept. 8, 1872; graduated from

Harvard College, 1894; Treasurer and Vice-Pesident of the Fall
River, Mass., Bleachery since 1899; the son of Spencer Borden
of Fall River, Mass., and of Effie Brooks of Salem, Ohio.

(10) BLANCHE BUTLER BORDEN b. April 27, 1902.

(10) SPENCER BORDEN, 3d, b. Sept. 6, 1903; d. Feb. 2, 1909.

(10) JOAN BORDEN b. Sept. 14, 1906.

(10) AMES BORDEN b. Nov. 23, 1908.

(9) BLANCHE AMES b. Feb. 18, 1878; graduated from
Roger's Hall School, Lowell, Mass., 1895; and from Smith College, 1899; m. May 15, 1900, Oakes Ames of North Easton,
Mass.; b. North Easton, Mass., Sept. 26, 1874; graduated from
Hopkinson's School, Boston, Mass., 1894, and from Harvard
College with A.B., 1898; A.M. 1899; Assistant in Botany at Harvard College, 1899-1900; Instructor in Botany, Harvard College,
since 1900; Assistant Director of the Botanic Garden of Harvard
College, 1899-1909; Director of the Harvard College Botanic
Garden, 1909. The son of Oliver Ames of North Easton, Mass.,
and of Annie Coffin (Ray) Hadwen of Nantucket, Mass.

(10) PAULINE AMES b. Oct. 21, 1901.

(10) OLIVER AMES b. May 20, 1903.

(10) AMYAS AMES b. June 15, 1906.

(9) ADELBERT AMES, JR., b. Aug. 19, 1880.

(9) JESSIE AMES b. N. Y. City, Nov. 2, 1882.

* * *

(7) OLIVE W. AMES b. Feb. 13 (17), 1810; d. Feb. 27, 1847;
she was the 1st wife of Samuel Rankin of Thomaston, and afterwards of South Thomaston, Me., who was a storekeeper and
lime manufacturer; m. April 7, 1831; this family lived at East
Thomaston, Me. He b. Feb. 11, 1810; son of Samuel Rankin
and Elizabeth Jameson. He m. (2d) July 1, 1849, Lucy Gay.

(8) ALBERT RANKIN d. about 1880; unm.; served in U. S.
Army.

* * *

(7) CHARLOTTE S. AMES b. Feb. 14, 1812; d. Mch. 27, 1834;
m. Apr. 7, 1831, Hiram Brewster b. Thomaston, Me., May 22,
1808; d. Rockland, Me., May 9, 1878; ship-caulker; (he m. 2d
Feb. 16, 1836, Mrs. Sarah (Cooper) Sleeper; widow of Nathaniel
Sleeper; no children of this second marriage.)

(8) MELVINA AMANDA BREWSTER b. Mch. 4, 1832; d. Apr.
12, 1867; m. Woodbury P. Dyer, b. S. Portland, Me., Oct. 18,

1832; d. Apr. 12, 1867; he was of Rockland, Me., but after his marriage the family removed to Portland, Me.; a boat builder.

(9) HIRAM W. DYER b. Rockland, Me., June 15, 1854; florist at S. Portland, Me.; m. 1875 Alwilda Oliver b. Georgetown, Me., Feb. 14, 1856; the daughter of James Oliver and Lydia—;

(10) MILDRED O. DYER b. Jan. 17, 1876.

(10) LENORE B. DYER b. Nov. 8, 1878.

(10) LUCY P. DYER b. Mch. 12, 1889.

(9) EVA S. DYER b. Rockland, Me., Oct. 7, 1859; m. Mch. 15, 1889, Albert A. Cole of S. Portland, Me.; b. Freeport, Me., Dec. 3, 1853; Cole Brothers, Groceries, Hardware, Paints, Oils, etc., S. Portland, Me.; the son of Rotheus Cole and Margaret A. ————.

(10) ROTHEUS P. COLE b. Mch. 24, 1890.

(10) MARGARET M. COLE b. Nov. 3, 1896.

(10) HIRAM COLE b. Sept. 9, 1899.

(8) JOHN JARVIS BREWSTER b. Rockland, Me., Dec. 21, 1833; lost at sea July 6, 1861; mate of a merchant ship; m. Nov. 26, 1860, Emeline M. Mariner, b. Jan. 13, 1836. "J. J. Brewster was one of nature's noblemen."

* * *

(7) LUCY PERRY AMES, the fifth child of John Ames and Hannah Perry, b. July 7, 1814; d. Feb. 14, 1896; m. Mch. 5, 1835, Captain Nathaniel Crockett b. Rockland, Me., June 17, 1813; d. June 20, 1876; the son of Jonathan Crockett. He followed the sea all his life, being Captain of various vessels for about twenty-three years, carrying freight and passengers between Rockland, Me., and Boston, Mass. He was an honest, temperate, and noble man, and highly respected by all who knew him. His devoted wife made their Rockland, Me., home one of great joy and inspiration.

(8) PEMBROKE SOMERSET CROCKETT b. East Thomaston, Me., July 9, 1836; d. at Charlestown, Mass., May 6, 1909, after a very brief illness from pneumonia. "His passing away marked the life of a man into whose seventy-two years had been pressed more of the variety in history than usually falls to the lot of one of his age. His early days were spent in many of the world's great ports, whither he had traveled on the old packet ship, Richard Robinson. At seventeen years he was mate of a Bark. Returning from a voyage to Hong Kong he left the sea for good,

after twenty years of service, and tried his fortunes in the Cali-
· fornian mines, remaining there about five years, a part of this
time being in the transportation business at Los Angeles, California. He then resided in Chicago, Ill., for ten years, in which
City he became a very faithful Christian. When he finally
returned to Rockland, Me., he brought an earnest letter of recom-
mendation to the First Baptist Church. Since Jan. 20, 1885, he
has been a highly esteemed citizen of Charlestown, Mass., for
many years having charge of the carpentry work at the State
Prison. Soon after his removal to Charlestown he was elected
Deacon of the Bunker Hill Baptist hurch, which office he held
with rare wisdom and fidelity until his decease, greatly endearing
himself to all members of that Church, and to all people with
whom he came in contact. His interest in the cause of religion
never wavered, and his years devoted to Christ gave a beautiful
example of constant Christianity. A very impressive Memorial
Service for him was held in the Bunker Hill Baptist Church of
Charlestown, Mass., Sunday evening, May 23, 1909. Earnest
tributes to his memory were given by Rev. Messrs. Benjamin R.
Harris, John Ward Moore, and John F. Barnes. He had united
with this Church by letter, March 25, 1887, and had been Deacon
since 1890. Services were also held at the home of his brother,
N. Cleveland Crockett, at Rockland, Me., where the interment
took place." Mr. Crockett m. Jan. 1, 1865, Angeline Wall b.
St. George, Me., Mch. 12, 1839; a woman of sturdy and noble
qualities; the daughter of Joseph Simmons Wall of St. George,
Me., and Nancy J. Kalloch of Warren, Me.

(9) GRACE HOWARD CROCKETT b. Chicago, Ill., Nov. 29,
1869; resides with her mother at 93 High St., Charlestown,
Mass.; graduated from Rockland, Me., schools; bookkeeper in
an insurance office at Charlestown, Mass.; a woman of noble
qualities; a member of the Bunker Hill Chapter, D. A. R., since
Apr. 1, 1897.

(8) EDGAR CROCKETT b. Dec. 6, 1837; d. 1907; a sailor until
the Civil War; then enlisted in Co. D, 2d Me. Regt. Berdon's
Sharpshooters; a very brave soldier in all his four years of service; he was Captain of Co. D when he was honorably discharged
from service; m. Frances Elizabeth Howard b. Rockland, Me.,
Apr. 24, 1844; d. Apr. 11, 1898.

(9) EDGAR HOWARD CROCKETT b. Nov. 2, 1874; resides 19
Pleasant St., Rockland, Me.; clerk in a hardware store; he was

an officer in the 1st Maine Vols., Co. H., in the Spanish American War; m. Eva Sylvester.

(10) Two Sons.

(8) NATHANIEL CLEVELAND CROCKETT b. Rockland, Me., Feb. 17, 1844; resides Corner of Main and Pleasant Sts., Rockland, Me.; schools of Rockland, Me.; Universalist; at first followed the sea; after his marriage he was engaged in the dry goods business for some twenty-two years; was also Proprietor of a grain store; is now a very successful carpenter; Knight of Pythias; m. Dec. 31, 1868, Emma Frances Robinson b. Rockland, Me., Sept. 30, 1846; Rockland schools; the daughter of Daniel Robinson and Mary Ann Fuller of Rockland, Me.; she now has charge of a Ladies' Furnishing Store. No children.

(8) CATHERINE EUDORA CROCKETT b. Rockland, Me., July 7, 1846; resides 30 High St., Charlestown, Mass.; m. Dec. 30, 1869, Jonathan A. Foye of Boston, Mass., b. Wiscasset, Me., and d. at Steele, North Dakota, Feb. 4, 1889; he was the proprietor of a dry goods store in the Maine towns, Wiscasset, Saco, and Waterville, and in Steele and Dawson, N. Dakota. No children.

* * *

(7) CAPTAIN JACKSON AMES b. Dec. 29, 1816; d. at Port au Prince, West Indies, Nov. 22, 1855; m. about 1838, Sally Thomas, b. 1818, the daughter of Seth Thomas and Hannah Dyer; as a widow she married Rev. Ichabod Sturdevant; her third husband was John Knowles; she lived for some time at Chesterville, Me.

(8) SAMUEL RANKIN AMES b. N. Haven, Me., Dec. 8, 1839; resides Proberta, Tehama County, California, having removed there from Sioux Falls, South Dakota; m. May 28, 1865, Lizzie Fowler Ames, sister of Nathan A., b. Feb. 28, 1840; of Hezekiah Ames and Sally Scofield.

(9) ELLA MERRILL AMES b. N. Haven, Me., June 3, 1866; for some time she resided at Sioux Falls, S. Dakota; m. Mch. 25, 1886, Edward Joseph South of Sioux Falls, South Dakota, b. May 1, 1863, who d. Nov. 24, 1898; farmer; steam engineer.

(10) MABEL SUSANNAH SOUTH b. Apr. 30, 1887.

(10) ADA FERNE SOUTH b. Apr. 21, 1890.

(10) ALICE ELIZABETH SOUTH b. Nov. 17, 1893.

(10) ROY AMES SOUTH b. Sept. 16, 1895.

(10) GLEN EDWARD SOUTH b. Apr. 12, 1897.

(9) ALBERT HOWARD AMES b. New Haven, Me., Nov. 27, 1869; resides Red Bluff, Calif.; m. Feb. 1, 1898, Emma Lewis.

(8) Oliver J. Conant Ames b. Sept. 7, 1842; killed by a fall from a horse, when twelve years old.

(8) Clara Nancy Ames b. N. Haven, Me., Jan. 26, 1845; resides Proberta, Calif.; m. Oct. 20, 1861, Nathan P. Ames, b. N. Haven, Me., Sept. 25, 1834; of Hezekiah Ames and 2d wife, Sally Scofield; a very successful raiser of fruit; moved from Maine to Iowa 1871; to Proberta, Calif., 1891.

(9) Otis M. Ames b. Nov. 3, 1864; fruit rancher and miner; married.

(9) Alice Ames b. Mch. 23, 1866; d. Oct. 26, 1878.

(9) Samuel R. Ames b. Sept. 12, 1879.

(8) Adna Ames b. Mch. 12, 1847; resides East Corinth, or Kenduskeag, Me.; m. Dec. 17, 1878, David Franklin Page.

(9) Blaine Ames Page b. Apr. 6, 1884.

(8) Augusta F. Ames b. 1850; d. June, 1876; m. 1871, David Page.

(9) John Douglass Page b. Oct., 1872; killed by a dynamite explosion at Butte, Montana, Jan., 1895.

(9) Adna Augusta Page b. May 11, 1874; m. 1893, Herbert G. Carmichel.

(10) Mabel Esther Carmichel b. 1895.

(10) John David Carmichel b. 1897.

(8) Jesse Ames b. May, 1852; lived Hanlonton, Iowa; to Oklahoma, 1902.

(8) Oliver Jackson Ames b. Nov., 1855; resides Proberta, Calif. Married 1889, Minnie Gilliam of Iowa.

(9) Five children—Gussie, Veda, Clinton, Alma, Alice, Clifford.

* * *

(7) David Ames, the seventh child of John Ames and Hannah Perry, b. N. Haven, Me., June 26, 1819; resides Northfield, Minn.; he received a fine education and taught school for fifteen years with good success; during the summers of these years when he was teaching he coasted from Rockland, Me., to N. Y. City, for a part of this time sailing a vessel of his own. In 1847 and 1850 he was a member of the Maine Legislature. In 1867 he removed to Northfield, Rice County, Minn., and was soon busily at work in his brother's flouring mill. He held several City and County offices up to 1893. Besides his town property he owns a farm of four hundred acres on Prairie Creek. M. Dec. 21, 1844,

Lucy Dyer of N. Haven, Me., b. May 9, 1822; the daughter of Ebenezer Dyer and Rebecca Young.

(8) CHARLOTTE BREWSTER AMES b. April 17, 1846; m. May 6, 1866, Reuben Carver Smith of Northfield, Minn., b. Dec. 25, 1841; farmer and merchant; son of Geo. W. Smith and Jane Calderwood Carver.

(9) LUCY ELLA SMITH b. Apr. 29, 1877; resides Northfield, Minn.

(9) JESSE DAVID SMITH b. July 21, 1879.

(9) GEORGE HAMLIN SMITH b. Ncv. 25, 1880; d. Sept. 22, 1881.

(9) JENNIE CELESTE SMITH b. July 1, 1886.

(8) HANNIBAL HAMLIN AMES b. Jan. 16, 1848; a miller at Hutchinson, Minn.; m. 1st, May 12, 1872, Mary Parker, b. Dec. 20, 1845, d. Feb. 12, 1888; m. 2d 1889, Edith A. Bromley, b. Apr. 27, 1865; children of second marriage:

(9) FLORENCE AMES b. July 2, 1890.

(9) RUTH AMES b. Mch. 20, 1892.

(8) JOHN BRADBURY AMES b. Sept. 16, 1851; fruit raiser at Proberta, Calif.; m. May 9, 1874, Henrietta Stocking; of Wm. Henry Stocking and Mary Ann Wallridge.

(9) CHARLOTTE BREWSTER AMES b. Nov. 16, 1876.

(9) CAROLINE LORELLA AMES b. July 5, 1878.

(9) FRANK STOCKING AMES b. Sept. 1, 1879.

(8) ARTHUR HALBERT AMES b. Fox Island, Me., Jan. 8, 1862; resides Hutchinson, Minn.; to Minn. 1866; Olivia and Terre Bonne; 1886-1894 in Hutchinson, Minn.; 1894-1900 in Northfield, Minn.; 1900 to present date in Hutchinson, Minn.; graduated from Northfield, Minn., High School, 1879; wheat buyer, bookkeeper, hardware merchant and flour mill owner; Postmaster at Terre Bonne, Minn., 1883-1884; served on the School Board at Northfield, Minn., 1899-1900; wife and children members of the Episcopal Church; K. P.; m. Sept. 14 1886, Caroline Jane Whitford b. Hampton, Dakota Co., Minn., Mch. 16, 1863; the daughter of James Harley Whitford and Catherine Maria Ludy, who resided in N. Y. State, Michigan, Kansas and Minnesota.

(9) MARGARET MARIA AMES b. Aug. 7, 1887; address Minneapolis, Minn.; graduated from Hutchinson, Minn., High School, 1905.

(9) HAZEL ELIZABETH AMES b. Sept. 23, 1889; resides Hutchinson, Minn.

* * * .

(7) HEZEKIAH AMES b. N. Haven, Me., June 28, 1821, d. Vinalhaven, Me., Aug. 20, 1898 (77); he was a very successful sea captain at North Haven, Me., until 1869, when he removed to Minnesota, returning to Vinalhaven, Me., in 1872; in the West he was a farmer; m. Andalusia P. Thomas b. 1825, d. Feb. 14, 1886.

(8) MARY NANCY AMES b. May 19, 1848; resides Vinalhaven, Maine; m. (1st) Nov. 7, 1864, Ulmer Andrew Brown, b. North Haven, Me., Sept. 6, 1841, d. Sept. 16, 1867; fisherman; a man of sturdy qualities; he died at Souris, P. E. I., having landed there from his vessel, ill from typhoid fever. He was the son of Horatio G. Brown of North Haven, Me., and of Philena Packard of South Thomaston, Me.; m. (2d) Jan. 31, 1871, Palmer Oscar Crandall b. May 5, 1842; resides Vinalhaven, Me.; harness maker.

Child of the first marriage of Mary Nancy Ames:

(9) JAMES OSMAN BROWN b. North Haven, Me., Aug. 20, 1865; resides North Haven, Me.; of fine help in securing records for this book; resided at Fort Atkinson, Ia., 1871-'72; Vinalhaven, Me., 1873-1887; since then at North Haven, Me.; a very successful boat builder; Free Mason; m. Nov. 26, 1885, Flora Annie Carver b. Vinalhaven, Me., June 12, 1865; the daughter of William Edward Carver, who is deceased, and of Sarah Jane Calderwood who resides at Vinalhaven, Me.

(10) FOY WELD BROWN b. Oct. 20, 1889; in 1910 a fine student in Y. M. C. A. School, Boston, Mass.

(10) VANIE EVELYN BROWN b. Aug. 24, 1892; graduated from North Haven, Me., High School, June, 1908; now attending the Burdette Business College, Boston, Mass.

(10) RUTH DORIS BROWN b. Feb. 15, 1904.

Children of the second marriage of Mary Nancy Ames, with Palmer Oscar Crandall:

(9) ADELBERT CLEVELAND CRANDALL b. Dec. 28, 1872; clerk in a clothing store, Lynn, Mass.; m. July 17, 1896, Eliza Des Roches.

(9) EMMA BLANCHE CRANDALL b. Dec. 28, 1872; resides 11 A Chase St., Lynn, Mass.

(9) ANNIE FRANCES CRANDALL b. July 29, 1875; resides North Haven, Me.; m. Richard A. Smith who d. Sept. 21, 1898; m. (2d) Mr. Eaton. Child of the first marriage:

(10) CORA MAY SMITH b. Mch. 4, 1898.

(9) MAUD ELIZABETH CRANDALL b. Vinalhaven, Me., May 10, 1878; resides West Quincy, Mass.; has lived in the Maine towns, Portland and Hallowell; at Hardwick, Vt., and at East Milton, Mass.; graduated from Vinalhaven, Me., High School, June, 1896; m. Oct. 5, 1896, James McKinley Ward, b. Bethel, N. Carolina, Apr. 18, 1874; stone cutter; Red Man; Odd Fellow; Knight of Pythias; the son of Benjamin Franklin Ward and Julia Elizabeth Taylor of Bethel, North Carolina.

(10) DORA ELIZABETH WARD b. Vinalhaven, Me., Mch. 26, 1897.

(10) JAMES FRANKLIN WARD b. Hardwick, Vt., Jan. 7, 1905.

(9) HEZEKIAH WELLS CRANDALL b. Vinalhaven, Me., July 4, 1880; resides Pasadena, Calif.; has lived at Rockland and Camden, Me.; Lynn, Mass.; Westerly, R. I.; Westminster, Vt.; Stonington, Me.; Islesboro, Me.; Revere, Mass.; and Long Island, N. Y., towns, Port Jefferson, Hemstead, and Garden City; also lived for short periods in Boston, Mass.; N. Y. City; St. Joseph and St. Louis, Mo.; Salt Lake City, Utah; Jacksonville, Florida; Los Angeles, Calif.; etc., etc. Graduated from Vinalhaven, Me., High School, 1899; carpenter and builder; club chef; attends the Baptist Church; member of I. O. O. F., Star of Hope, No. 42, Vinalhaven, Me.

(9) OSCAR BRADFORD CRANDALL b. Mch. 29, 1882.

(9) WALTER MIDKIFF CRANDALL b. Mch. 29, 1884; resides 11 A Chase St., Lynn, Mass.

(9) BERTHA MILDRED CRANDALL b. May 1, 1888.

(8) SARAH FRANCES AMES b. Sept. 12, 1850, d. Aug. 15, 1898 (47-11-'3); m. Dec. 15, 1867, Leander Bradford Smith b. North Haven, Me., Nov. 7, 1843; butcher at Vinalhaven, Me.; the son of George Washington Smith and Jane Cleaver.

(9) BERTHA ETTA SMITH b. Oct. 12, 1870; resides Rockland, Me.; member of the Methodist Church; m. Aug. 8, 1894, Charles Edwin Meservy b. Appleton, Me., Mch. 25, 1856; lived Vinalhaven, Me., 1870-1894; at S. Thomaston, Me., 1894-1910; address Rockland, Me., lawyer; Judge of the Probate Court of Knox County, Me., for eight years; he graduated from the Coburn Classical School, 1877; from Colby College, 1881; ad-

mitted to Knox County, Me., Bar, Sept., 1884; Superintendent of Schools at S. Thomaston, Me., several times; Collector and Treasurer of S. Thomaston, Me., since 1900; the son of William Henry Meservy and Clarinda Ripley.

(9) MINNIE CARVER SMITH b. Vinalhaven, Me., Dec. 28, 1872; address, Rockland, Me.; graduated from Rockland, Me., schools.

(9) ORRIN FREDERICK SMITH b. Mch. 19, 1877; resides Rockland, Me.; graduated from Vinalhaven, Me., High School; m. Aug. 1, 1905, Cora Hopkins of Vinalhaven, Me.; no children.

(9) Infant daughter b. Feb., 1880, d. Nov., 1880.

(8) ORRIN BRADFORD AMES b. Sept. 2, 1855; carries on his father's farm at Vinalhaven, Me.; graduated from Vinalhaven, Me., High School; and from Rockland, Me., High School; m. Jan. 11, 1879, Ella Estelle Carver, b. Dec. 2, 1859.

(9) LUCY EMMA AMES b. June 30, 1880, d. Sept. 20, 1883.

(9) LAVON THOMAS AMES b. Vinalhaven, Me., Jan. 26, 1882; resides 127 Rotch St., New Bedford, Mass.; was at Vinalhaven, Me., until 1900; then to Boston, Mass., and entered the wholesale shoe trade; Clark-Hutchinson Company, boots, shoes, rubbers, and findings; 111, 113, 115 and 117 Federal St., Boston, Mass.; schools of Vinalhaven, Me.; member of I. O. O. F.; and of United Travelers; m. Dec. 25, 1896, Mary Elizabeth Robb b. Medford, Mass., Dec. 24, 1881; graduated from Medford, Mass., High School; the daughter of William David Robb and Augusta Baker Flood.

(10) MARJORIE AUGUSTA AMES b. New Bedford, Mass., Aug. 17, 1908.

(9) CLYDE OSMOND AMES b. Mch. 6, 1887; m. May 14, 1910, Bina C. Stone.

(9) CARL LESTER AMES b. Feb. 13, 1888.

(9) CHARLES M. AMES b. Feb. 2, 1897.

* * *

(7) OTIS AMES, the ninth child of John Ames and Hannah Perry, b. Oct. 27, 1823, d. in youth.

* * *

(7) NANCY PERRY AMES b. July 30, 1826, d. Feb. 25, 1866; m. Dec. 20, 1847, Captain Oliver J. Conant of East Thomaston, Me., b. Dec. 14, 1825; resides 144 Union St., Rockland, Me.; he was a very successful merchant from quite an early age until the

beginning of the Civil War; he then enlisted in the Army; after close of the War was Post Master at Rockland, Me., for some time.

(8) ETTA O. CONANT b. Jan. 28, 1857; resides 83 Gardner St., Allston, Mass.; m. Sept. 15, 1881, Nathan D. Clark of Boston, Mass.; b. Nov. 23, 1856, d. Apr. 10, 1896; he was a wholesale boot and shoe merchant at Boston, Mass.; firm, Clark and Hutchinson.

(9) FREDERICK CONANT CLARK b. June 26, 1882.

(8) ANNIE O. CONANT b. Jan. 4, 1860; resides Rockland, Me.

CHAPTER FOUR.

THE RECORDS OF LUCY PERRY AND BENJAMIN THOMAS.

* * *

(6) LUCY PERRY, the sixth child of Captain John Perry and Lucy Wooster, b. Apr. 13, 1785, d. Feb. 20, 1851; resided at Rockland, Me.; a woman of the noblest qualities; m. Jan. 8, 1806, Capt. Benjamin Thomas, who was lost at sea on the schooner Thomas, Sept. 15, 1819; a very enterprising and successful Captain, son of Benjamin Thomas.

* * *

(7) ROXANA THOMAS b. Apr. 15, 1808; when last heard from she was living at Vinalhaven, Me., in wonderful vigor for one of her years; she was a most helpful neighbor in every community where she lived; m. Mch., 1830, Captain Howland Dyer, a man who was very faithful in every duty which life presented to him; he was a successful sea Captain until 1832; then was Captain of the U. S. Revenue Cutter at Castine, Me.; on Feb. 22, 1832, while firing salutes for Washington's birthday a gun burst and broke both his legs; after this he had charge of Brown's Head Lighthouse until President Johnson removed him; he lived but a short time after this."

(8) ARDELLE DE FOREST DYER b. July 6, 1831; m. (1st) at Newburyport, Mass., Jan. 10, 1848, Daniel P. Lee, b. Apr. 15, 1825, d. at Havana, Cuba, Mch. 14, 1855; seaman; m. (2d) Apr. 19 1857, Theophilus Arey b. Nov. 11, 1833; stone cutter.

Children of the first marriage:

(9) ADELIA HELEN LEE b. Rockland, Me., June 14, 1849; resides 45 River St., Hyde Park, Mass.; m. Sept. 12, 1870, George Edward Billings.

(9) FRANCES THOMAS LEE b. Newburyport, Mass., Sept. 24, 1854, d. Sept. 16, 1870, at Vinalhaven, Me.

(9) MAHALA ADELAIDE LEE b. Sep. 12, 1856; m. (1st) Mr. Ames; m. (2d) Samuel Cobb; resides Vinalhaven, Me.

Child of the second marriage:

(9) NATHAN DYER AREY b. June 18, 1874; m. Dec. 24, 1894, Maud Garrett, b. Nov. 3, 1874.

(10) HIRAM AUSTIN AREY b. Mch. 10, 1896.

———

(8) ROBERT A. DYER b. Oct. 14, 1835; fisherman at Vinalhaven, Me.; m. July 19, 1857, Mahala Calderwood, b. Oct. 18, 1836; the daughter of Matthew Calderwood and Peggy C. ———; no children.

———

(8) JAMES C. DYER b. Oct. 4, 1839, d. June 24, 1891; fisherman; m. (1st) Sabra N. Mills; m. (2d) Apr. 4, 1877, Ada Spencer Mills b. Sept. 7, 1850.

(9) LUELLA SABRA DYER b. June 5, 1878.

(9) ROXANA ADA DYER b. Apr. 3, 1886, d. Mch. 1, 1887.

———

(8) NATHAN T. DYER b. Oct. 4, 1839; fisherman at N. Haven, Me.; m. Jan., 1863, Catherine Crockett.

(9) WILLIAM L. M. DYER b. Nov., 1863, d. 1869.

(9) WILLIAM DYER b. 1874; m. Mary J. Farwell.

(10) Child.

———

(8) CAPT. STEPHEN HATCH DYER b. Apr. 3, 1843 (1844?); m. Jan. 29, 1868, Emma L. Philbrook, b. Oct. 7, 1849; the daughter of Joel Philbrook and Mary F. ———; no children.

———

(8) ALDANA C. DYER b. Feb. 1, 1847; m. (1st) May 31, 1865, David B. Thomas, b. July 27, 1839, d. Nov. 3, 1898; seaman; the son of William Thomas and Charlotte Smith; m. (2d) Leander Smith. "This family has the little iron kettle which belonged to Captain John Perry and was used by him the day that he shot the Englishmen."

Children of the first marriage:

(9) OMAR L. THOMAS b. Feb. 23, 1868; unm.

(9) CHARLES H. THOMAS b. Oct. 16, 1872; unm.

(9) HEHRY L. THOMAS b. May 17, 1878.

———

(8) AURANIA DYER b. Apr. 17, 1849; resides 141 West 105th S., N. Y. City; a woman of sterling qualitesi and of great help in

the writing of this Perry History; m. Nov. 22, 1867, Thomas
Hanley, b. Passage, W. Ireland, Feb. 1, 1842; the son of Jere-
miah Hanley and Margaret—, who are deceased. Mr. Thomas
Hanley came to America in Apr., 1856; he lived at Cumberland
Centre, Me., until May 1, 1861, when he enlisted in the Civil War,
Company A, 1st Me. Regt.; and was honorably discharged Aug.
5, 1861; re-enlisted in Co. A., 10th Me. Regiment, for two years,
at Portland, Me., May 7, 1863; re-enlisted in Co. E., 29th Maine
Regiment for three years, Aug. 7, 1863, and was honorably discharged at Hilton Head, S. C., June 21, 1866; Mr. Hanley was
one of the nineteen men who went through three Regiments.
John M. Gould in his history of these three Regiments says,
"First Sergeant Thomas Hanley has fairly earned the honor of
having done the most service of any enlisted man in the Regiments. He was faithful and honest, a thorough soldier, and a
good Sergeant. His days were not spent in whiling away his
time, but in doing genuine service for the nation. He was in
every fight, skirmish, and march, of his Regiment and Company,
and never lost a day by sickness during active service, but stayed
by his comrades from first to last." Since the close of the War
he has done all that he could for his country. He has long been
an Engineer in the Lighthouse Department, being stationed in
the Government Yard at Staten Island, N. Y.

   (9) FRANCES LEE HANLEY b. Aug. 31, 1868.

----

   (8) CHARLES O. DYER b. May 3, 1852; resides Vinalhaven,
Me.; a very successful farmer; m. July 7, 1874, Isadore Thayer.
   (9) AUREAMA DYER b. Aug. 22, 1875.
   (9) HUGH A. DYER b. Oct. 16, 1877; in May, 1898, he
enlisted in the U. S. Navy and was discharged in Oct. of that
year.
   (9) HALLIE C. DYER b. July 7, 1881.
   (9) BESSIE M. DYER b. June 8, 1883.
   (9) HARRY A. DYER b. July 20, 1887.
   (9) FLORENCE L. DYER b. Oct. 26, 1889.
   (9) HANLEY T. DYER b. July 11, 1893.
   (9) HESTER C. DYER b. Feb. 7, 1894.
   (9) SUSAN B. DYER b. Dec. 19, 1897.

----

   (8) HENRY W. DYER b. Sept. 12, 1855; resides North Haven,
Me.; m. Apr. 4, 1877, Elvira Crockett b. Oct. 7, 1850.

(9) LUELLA SABRA DYER b. Rockland, Me., Jan. 5, 1878; resides 2003 2d Ave., Seattle, Washington.

(9) CORA ADA DYER b. Feb. 3, 1886, d. Mch. 1, 1887.

* * *

(7) JULIA GLOVER THOMAS, the second child of Benjamin Thomas and Lucy Perry, b. North Haven, Me., Nov. 24, 1809, d. Rockland, Me., Sept. 4, 1897; studied in the schools of N. Haven and East Thomaston, Me.; a woman of grand helpfulness; m. Dec. 25, 1831, Willard Sterling Blackington, b. East Union, Me., Nov. 11, 1804, d. Mch. 1, 1883; a very worthy citizen of Rockland, Me.; a very successful Inspector of Lime; a member of the Odd Fellows for many years; the son of James Wight Blackington, a Universalist, and of Hannah Keene.

----

(8) OSCAR EATON BLACKINGTON b. East Thomaston, Me., Jan. 6, 1833; resides Rockland, Me., where he has been a very successful clothing salesman for over thirty-five years; at one time engaged in the livery business; has also lived at E. Thomaston, Me.; in Vinalhaven, Me., 1861-1863; in Jonesport, Me., 1863-1867; since then at Rockland, Me., he is a Free Mason of high standing; an enthusiastic and helpful citizen; has served on the Rockland City Council; Tax Assessor; Clerk of Registrar; Chairman of the city board, etc.; m. (1st) June 17, 1862, Susan Bibber Mansfield b. Jonesport, Me., Feb. 7, 1840; d. Sept. 6, 1884; the daughter of Edward A. Mansfield and Louise Sawyer who resided at Jonesport and Rockland, Me.; m. (2d) Sept. 1, 1885, Julia M. Withington, b. Rockland, Me., May 16, 1860; the daughter of Ephraim Withington and Dolly Goodhill Miller who lived at Camden and Rockland, Me. Children of the first marriage.

(9) JESSE MILLS BLACKINGTON b. Jonesport, Me., Apr. 7, 1863; resides Union, Me.; has lived in the Maine towns, Rockland, Mechanic Falls, etc., and in Boston, Mass.; Rockland, Me., schools; Universalist in faith; member of I. O. O. F.; a very successful traveling salesman; m. June 26, 1884, Martha Burgess Teague b. Warren, Me., Aug. 4, 1866; graduated from Warren, Me., High School; the daughter of James H. Teague and of Ellen M. Henderson of Warren, Me.

(10) CLARENCE SAFFORD BLACKINGTON b. July 24, 1885; resides Bath, Me.; graduated from Mechanic Falls, Me., High

School, June, 1901; druggist; m. Aug., 1909, Mildred Hayes of Bath, Me.

(10) OSCAR EATON BLACKINGTON b. Dec. 28, 1887; resides Corvallis, Washington; student in Oregon University.

(9) ALBERT T. BLACKINGTON b. Jonesport, Me., July 5, 1866; a very successful dry goods salesman and manufacturer at Rockland, Me.; m. Oct. 24, 1892, Ada Johnson Simonton b. Rockland, Me., Jan. 8, 1867; of Frederic James Simonton and Flora J. Adams; no children.

(9) RALPH HARVEY BLACKINGTON b. Rockland, Me., Dec. 20, 1867, d. Aug. 22, 1900; always lived in Rockland, Me.; graduated from the University of Maine; chemist; also very successful in the boot and shoe business; m. Jan. 22, 1896, Jessie Burkett b. Thomaston, Me., Aug. 15, 1875; graduated from Thomaston, Me., High School; the daughter of Isaac Burkett of Thomaston, M. (She m. (2) Ralph Tibbetts of Rockport, Me.)

(10) MAURICE BLACKINGTON b. June 25, 1897.

(9) LUIE ELDEMAR BLACKINGTON b. July 16, 1875; m. June 22, 1903, Ernestine Clemice Cunningham.

(10) CLEMICE MANSFIELD BLACKINGTON.

Children of the second marriage of Oscar E. Blackington, with Julia Withington.

(9) SUE VIRGINIA BLACKINGTON b. Aug. 12, 1886; resides Rockland, Me.; m. July 5, 1905, John F. Whitney, who d. Aug. 26, 1908.

(9) KENNETH WILLIAM BLACKINGTON b. Mch. 27, 1888; resides Rockland, Me.; clerk in his father's store; graduated from Rockland, Me., High School, June 16, 1906.

(9) CARL ADAMS BLACKINGTON b. July 6, 1890; graduated from Rockland, Me., High School, June 14, 1909.

(9) RUTH BROWNIE BLACKINGTON b. Nov. 24, 1891; student in Rockland, Me., High School.

---

(8) LUCY KATHERINE BLACKINGTON b. Oct. 16, 1834, d. Jan. 9, 1890; resided in the Maine towns, Dexter, Bangor and Rockland; studied in a Rockland, Me., Private School; a very faithful member of the Congregational Church; m. Mch. 5, 1859, John Henry Additon b. Dexter, Me., Apr. 27, 1838, d. Sept. 23, 1882; a fine traveling salesman and merchant; member of the First Baptist Church, Rockland, Me.; the son of David Additon b.

Leeds, Me., June 17, 1799, d. Mch. 21, 1861; m. Feb. 25, 1819, Matilda Preston b. Sept. 8, 1797, d. Apr. 27 1862. (For Additon Records write Mrs. Sarah J. Ham, 19 High St., Lewiston, Me.; she is the only living child of her father's family.)

(9) HARVEY FAIRFIELD ADDITON b. Rockland, Me., Feb. 16, 1871; for some time the proprietor of a book and stationery store; 1910, traveling salesman from Indianapolis, Ind.; he and his wife members of the Woodruff Place Baptist Church; m. Aug. 6, 1894, Alice Emery b. S. Thomaston, Me., Mch. 10, 1870; the daughter of Bradford Alden Emery and Elizabeth Octavia Maddocks, who resided at Thomaston, Me.

(10) ELIZABETH EMERY ADDITON b. Aug. 5, 1895.

(10) PHYLLIS HOPE ADDITON b. July 18, 1896.

(10) MARGARET CRIE ADDITON b. Aug. 11, 1897, d. Nov. 4, 1901.

(10) RUTH MADDOCKS ADDITON b. Dec. 29, 1898.

(10) FAITH KATHERINE ADDITON b. Feb. 1, 1904.

---

(8) MARY THERESA BLACKINGTON b. E. Thomaston, now Rockland, Me., Feb. 11, 1838; d. July 1, 1910; resided Lincolnville, Me.; has also lived in Maine towns, Rockland, North Haven and Warren; she and her husband are faithful members of the Camden, Me., Baptist Church; m. Oct. 22, 1859, Hanson Albert Mills b. Vinalhaven, Me., May 19, 1829; fisherman, mail carrier, and merchant; Free Mason; the son of Moses Mills and Sabra Calderwood of Calderwood's Neck, Vinalhaven, Me.

---

(8) COLONEL OLIVER NELSON BLACKINGTON b. Rockland, Me., Mch. 14, 1840; resides Augusta, Me.; in that City since 1872; graduated from Rockland, Me., schools, 1856; he and his wife very helpful members of the Episcopal Church; member of G. A. R.; Free Masons; Order of Red Men; a very highly respected citizen; enlisted in the Civil War at Rockland, Me., Apr. 24, 1861, in Company C, 4th Maine Regiment Infantry; mustered out at New Orleans, La., Nov. 30, 1866; Corporal, Nov., 1861; Sergeant, Aug., 1862; Sergeant Major of the 4th Maine Volunteer Infantry, Mch. 1st, 1863; Captain, Aug. 29, 1863; Major, Feb. 26, 1865; Lieutenant Colonel, Dec. 24, 1865; U. S. Infantry. He bravely took part in the following engagements: First Bull Run, Yorktown, Williamsburg, Fair Oaks or

Seven Pines, Gains Mills, Savage Station, White Oak Swamp, Glendale, Malvern Hill; continuous seven days' fighting in front of Richmond, 2d Bull Run, Chantilly, Fredericksburg; Port Hudson May 27, 1863; Second Assault, June 14, 1863. Mr. Blackington was Councilman of Ward 3, Rockland, Me., 1870; Chairman of the Board of Registration, Parish Natchitoches, La., under Reconstruction Laws, 1867-1868. Is now Messenger for U. S. Pension Agency; and was previously a very successful commercial traveler and proprietor of a livery stable. M. Nov. 19, 1865, Matilda Welch Worrall b. Philadelphia, Pa., Jan. 6, 1849; graduated from Coats St. High School, Philadelphia; the daughter of Nathan Harper Worrall and ▄Matilda Louise Duffield of Frankford, Pa.

(9) CYRUS HARTWELL BLACKINGTON b. New Orleans, La., Dec. 24, 1866; resides 1334 Blue Hill Ave., Mattapan, Mass.; resided New Orleans, La., 1866-Apr., 1868; Rockland, Me., 1868-1874; East Winthrop, Me., 1874-1876; Manchester, Me., 1876-1879; Augusta, Me., 1879-1899; a very energetic and successful salesman; he and his wife are members of the Episcopal Church; First Lieutenant of 1st Maine Volunteer Infantry, War with Spain; member Sons of Veterans; Free Mason; m. Oct. 17, 1894, Florence Mertie May b. Augusta, Me., Sept. 24, 1869; schools of Augusta, Me.; the daughter of John H. May and of Ellen Lena Guild of Augusta, Me.

(10) DONALD DUFFIELD BLACKINGTON b. Augusta, Me., Sept. 28, 1895.

(9) JULIUS FAIRFIELD BLACKINGTON b. July 5, 1868, d. Dec. 12, 1876.

(9) HELEN GERTRUDE BLACKINGTON b. Feb. 5, 1872; resides Augusta, Me.; a faithful member of the Episcopal Church; graduated from Cony High School, Augusta, Me.; m. Jan. 13, 1902, Newman Hubert Athoe, b. Merve, England, May, 1872; graduated from Oxford College of Music; Proprietor of Lime Rock Company.

(10) MARY GWENDOLYN ATHOE b. Jan. 22, 1903.

(10) DORIS BLACKINGTON ATHOE b. Oct. 7, 1905.

(10) JOHN KENNETH ATHOE b. Nov. 22, 1906.

(10) OLIVER NELSON ATHOE b. Apr. 4, 1908.

(9) WILLARD STARLING BLACKINGTON b. July 25, 1873, d.

Feb. 6, 1897; a member of the Episcopal Church; a successful photographer at Fresno, California.

————

(8) LYDIA JANE BLACKINGTON b. Rockland, Me., May 16, 1842; resides Dover, Me.; a woman of sturdy and helpful character; studied in Rockland, Me., schools; also in private schools; formerly a member of the Universalist Church, now a member of the Christian Science Church; m. Jan. 1, 1860, John Fairfield Fogler b. Union, Me., May 24, 1839, d. Apr. 29, 1898; he went to Rockland, Me., when seventeen years of age and remained there until his death; studied in the schools of Union, Me., and graduated from Warren, Me., Academy; merchant; member of Clarmont Commandery of Knights Templar; a member of the Universalist Church; a man of noble qualities; the son of Charles Fogler and Martha Carroll who resided in Union, Me.

(9) MARTHA EDITH FOGLER b. Rockland, Me., Feb. 3, 1861; resides Dover, Me.; lived Rockland, Me., 1861-1889; at Dover, Me., since 1889; studied in the schools of Rockland, Me., and one year in the Private School of Mr. Woodbridge of Rockland, Me.; a member of the Christian Science Church; m. Oct. 16, 1889, William Chalmers Woodbury b. Dover, Me., Dec. 15, 1857; graduated from Foxcroft, Me., Academy; Treasurer of the Piscataquis Savings Bank, Dover, Me.; Free Mason; Treasurer of Piscataquis County, Me., 1884-1888; the son of Charles H. B. Woodbury and Lucinda B. Tower of Dover, Me.

(10) PAULINE WOODBURY b. Dover, Me., Apr. 9, 1893; graduated from the schools of Dover, Me., and from Foxcroft, Me., Academy.

(10) CHARLES FAIRFIELD WOODBURY b. Dover, Me., Feb. 19, 1899.

(9) MARY CROCKETT FOGLER b. Rockland, Me., Feb. 5, 1871; resides Dover, Me.; resided in Rockland, Me., until her marriage; graduated from Rockland, Me., High School, June, 1888; she and her husband are members of the Christian Science Church; m. Sept. 7, 1899, Caleb Henry Cushing b. Sebec, Me., 1869; graduated from Foxcroft, Me., Academy, 1886; manufacturer of the Perfection Dyes; Treasurer of Piscataquis County, Me., 1900-1906; Trustee of Piscataquis Savings Bank, Dover, Me.; Past Commander of G. A. R. Post; the son of Major Wain-

wright Cushing and of Flora A. McIntire of Foxcroft, Me.; these
parents resided at Foxcroft, Me.

(8) OLIVE RANKIN BLACKINGTON b. Nov. 11, 1847; resides
Rockland, Me.; graduated from Rockland, Me., schools; m. Apr.
26, 1866, Haford S. Moor, who is a jeweller at Rockland, Me.;
Odd Fellow; no children.

(8) JERUSHA BLACKINGTON b. Dec. 18, 1849; resides Rockland, Me.; graduated from Rockland, Me., schools; a very helpful member of the Universalist Church; m. Feb. 17, 1870, Ed-
mond B. Hastings b. Hope, Me., Apr. 26, 1845; studied in the
schools of Hope and Union, Me.; a very successful dry goods
merchant at Rockland, Me.; on the City Council 1875-1876; Free
Mason; member of the Elks; the son of Erwin Hastings and
Elizabeth Walker of Hope and Union, Me.
   (9) ALBERT MILLS HASTINGS b. Dec. 8, 1870; in the dry
goods business; graduated from the Maine State College.

(8) CAROLINE JANETTE BLACKINGTON b. Rockland, Me.,
Dec. 8, 1852; d. June 30, 1875; graduated from Rockland, Me.,
High School, 1871; a very successful teacher.

(8) ANNA BELLE BLACKINGTON b. Rockland, Me., Nov. 3,
1854; resides Rockland, Me.; Rockland, Me., schools; m. June
18, 1873, Charles Thorndike Spear, b. Rockland, Me., July 15,
1850; graduated from Farmington, Me., schools; florist; the son
of Alfred K. Spear and Nancy Thorndike of Rockland, Me.
   (9) ALFRED SPEAR died in infancy.
   (9) HAZEL M. SPEAR; resides 180 Middle St., Rockland, Me.
   (9) CARUS THORNDIKE SPEAR b. Rockland, Me., June 5, 1885;
has resided in Bangor, Me., since Oct. 10, 1909; a very successful commercial traveler; he and his wife members of the Universalist Church; member of Odd Fellows; Royal Elks, and of the
United Commercial Travelers; m. June 22, 1907, Bessie May Gilson b. Gardiner, Me., May 4, 1883; graduated from Rockland,
Me., High School, 1902; the daughter of W. Fred Manson and

adopted daughter of John Henry Gilson of Rockland, Me. Before her marriage she was a very successful milliner.

(10) DOROTHY FARWELL SPEAR b. July 1, 1908.

* * *

(7) LYDIA SMITH THOMAS b. Vinalhaven, Me., Mch. 13, 1814; d. Nov. 12, 1910; resided Rockland, Me.; though past ninety-six years of age she was bright, cheerful and helpful; her entire life has been filled with noble services for humanity and with good works for all about her; she is greatly respected and beloved; since her early childhood Rockland, Me., has been her home; and trips to Kansas and California have given her great pleasure and a wider scope for her helpful words and deeds; she studied in the schools of E. Thomaston and Rockland, Me.; she and her husband very faithful members of the First Baptist Church; m. Apr., 1833, Stephen Nelson Hatch b. Eastport, Me., Jan. 15, 1812, d. Rockland, Me., Sept. 2, 1876; schools of Eastport and E. Thomaston, Me.; a very successful harness maker, merchant and banker. "He pursued his various avocations quietly and persistently; was a very patriotic citizen; was first a Whig, and then a staunch Republican; was temperate in all his habits; was earnest and zealous for the best in all lines of life; he was tall and commanding in stature, and as straight in body as in thought. He was the son of Stephen Hatch who resided at Eastport and Rockland, Me. He was one of a family of ten children all but two of whom have passed to the beyond. Except for the two years, 1850-1852, spent in California, he resided in Rockland, Me., from his early boyhood." The children were born at East Thomaston, now Rockland, Me.

---

(8) LUCY HELEN HATCH b. Feb. 28, 1834; resides Fresno, California; a woman of sturdy and helpful character; resided Ottawa, Kansas, 1864-1870; Leavenworth, Kansas, 1872-1875; San Francisco, California, 1875-1878; Rockland, Me., 1878-1879; at Fresno, California, since 1879; Rockland, Me., schools and studied in Mount Holyoke Seminary, 1852-1855; a very successful teacher in Rockland, Me., public schools, at the University, Ottawa, Kansas; Maplewood Seminary, Leavenworth, Kansas; Clark Institute, San Francisco, Calif.; and gave twenty years of most faithful instruction at Fresno, Calif., 1879-1905; was very successful in the care of her fruit ranch of one hundred acres,

and a pioneer in the raisin industry; for several years past has been President of the Parlor Lecture Club.

---

(8) HANNAH ADELIA HATCH b. Oct. 25, 1835, d. Sept. 12, 1860; studied in private schools of Rockland, Me.; graduated from Charlestown, Mass., Female Seminary, 1856; "she was a very faithful and beloved teacher in Maine schools, and in the Seminary at Castleton, Vt., 1857; she was beautiful in person and character."

---

(8) JULIA ANN HATCH b. June 13, 1841, d. Mch. 11, 1842.

* * *

(7) HON. WILLIAM THOMAS, b. 1812, d. May 20, 1849; a tall, handsome, and brilliant man; a very prosperous merchant at Rockland Me.; State Senator in 1841; at the time of his death he was a candidate for Governor of Maine; m. Apr. 13, 1836, Hannah C. Robbins who m. (2d) Dr. Moses Sidney.

---

(8) FREDERIC THOMAS b. July 25, 1837, d. Nov. 3, 1837.

---

(8) ALBERT T. THOMAS b. Apr. 20, 1839, d. 1867.

---

(8) WILLIAM O. THOMAS b. June 20, 1842, d. in youth.

* * *

(7) JERUSHA G. THOMAS b. Mch. 20, 1816, d. Sept. 20, 1906; a woman of truly loving and noble nature, who brightened many homes and hearts in the community where she lived; m. Dec. 10, 1837, Nathan A. Farwell b. Unity, Me., Feb. 24, 1812, d. Dec. 10, 1893; the very efficient President of the Rockland, Me., Insurance Company; the son of Henry Farwell and Margaret ——— of Unity, Me. Obituary in a Rockland, Me., Journal: "He was of sturdy New England stock, His early life was cast along vigorous lines, and his education such as could be had in rural districts of that time. He taught schools at the age of twenty years, and two years later came to Rockland, Me., and from thence to East Thomaston, Me. On the busy industrial history of that growing town he made an

early impression. He was in trade; engaged in lime burning; built ships; and, at one time, commanded vessels in the coasting trade; afterwards sailing over deep waters in the Bark Epicure, in which he made much money. The Rockland Marine Insurance Company, one of the most successful institutions that Rockland has ever known, prospered under Mr. Farwell's management as President, paying large dividends, and making handsome returns on the final liquidation. He was the principal shareholder. He owned considerably in store and house property about the city of Rockland, notably the Farwell Opera House Block which he built with the late Capt. A. F. Ames. Originally a Whig in politics, he became a Republican on the organization of that party, and henceforth was a power in politics in that part of Maine. He was elected State Senator in 1861, and in 1863-1864 was President of the Senatorial body. In 1864 when William Pitt Fessenden resigned as U. S. Senator to accept the portfolio of Secretary of State, Governor Cony appointed Mr. Farwell to the vacancy, and he sat in National Senate amid the most distinguished compeers as a man that reflected the honor of the State of Maine that he represented. He was broad and noble in his political views, a man without fear, and without reproach, a politician of the Hannibal Hamlin type, the man whom he dearly loved and honored. His relatives who survive him are, Hon. Joseph Farwell of Unity, Me.; Mrs. Louisa Whitney of Newport, Me.; Mrs. Deborah A. Milliken of New Orleans, La.; the wife of Richard Milliken. In spite of the heavy snow storm which prevailed, the funeral of Mr. Farwell was a very large one. The Banks of the city were closed, and the Supreme Judicial Court adjourned its session, out of respect for this most worthy man. He had a noble, commanding form; he was alert and vigorous, and took a keen interest in affairs at home, and in the nation, and in the world. His mind embraced large things, and he kept in touch with the progress of events. His manner was kindly, and he was very tolerant of the views of others, and no spot of dishonor marred the uniform fairness of his character. He was liberal and just with poor men, and dispensed a generous bounty; daily doing many good deeds, and so unostentatiously that only the recipients knew what he had done; and thus the prayers of hundreds of grateful people followed him. He quietly fell asleep in death while his daughter was reading to him. This motto which was placed among the many beautiful flowers upon his casket was singularly appropriate, 'Thou shalt come to thy grave in full age, like as a shock of corn cometh in his season.'"

---

(8) MARY E. FARWELL d. in infancy Feb., 1839.

---

(8) CLARA M. FARWELL b. Jan. 18, 1840; resides Rockland, Me.; Recording Secretary of the W. C. T. U. of Maine, and a grand worker in the cause of truth.

---

(8) ANNIE ELIZA FARWELL b. July 16, 1841; resides Rockland, Me.; she and her husband are very helpful members of the Episcopal Church; m. Nov. 20, 1866, Edgar Alphonso Burpee b. Rockland, Me., Dec. 16, 1839; a very successful merchant; the son of Nathaniel Adams Burpee and Mary Partridge.

(9) FRANCES FARWELL BURPEE b. Feb. 2, 1870.
(9) ADA CARLETON BURPEE b. Aug. 11, 1872.

---

(8) FRANCES EATON FARWELL b. July 7, 1843; resides Boston, Mass.; a highly respected woman; m. Nov., 1883, Judge Walbridge Abner Field of Boston, Mass.; b. Springfield, Mass., Apr. 26, 1833, d. July 15, 1899. "His funeral services were held in the Second Congregational Church of Boston, Mass., Dr. Edward E. Hale and Rev. Dr. Donald officiating. He was preeminently a scholar. He graduated from Dartmouth College in 1855, and his reputation there was only equalled by Mr. Choate and Professor Putnam. He never failed in any exercise in his College course. At the Bar, in Congress, and upon the Bench, all who had to do with him felt that he had mastered all attainable knowledge on the subject under discussion. He was not a mere bookman; his mind presided over all that he read. He was of sterling New England ancestry. After studying law for awhile he returned to Dartmouth College to teach mathematics for a year, and then came to Boston to complete his legal studies, at Harvard Law School and in the office of Mr. Harvey Jewell. He was admitted to the Bar in 1860, and at once commenced his law practice in the office where he had fitted himself for work. He remained there until 1865 when he was successively Assistant U. S. District Attorney for Mass., for four years, under

Richard H. Dana and George S. Hilliard, and Assistant U. S. Attorney General under Hon. Rockwood Hoar for about a year. He returned to his old place of work in Boston, Mass., in 1870, was elected to Congress 1876, and held this seat until it was given to Mr. Dana by a Democratic Congress, Mch. 28, 1877. He was returned to his seat at the next Congressional election. He declined to again be a candidate, although strenuously urged to do so. His course in Congress was particularly satisfactory to his District. He was appointed to the Bench of the Supreme Court by Governor Long in February, 1881, and was made Chief Justice in 1890, when Chief Justice Morton resigned, by Governor Brackett. He served as a member of the Boston School Committee for two years, and was a member of the Boston Common Council for three years, and was also a member of the Massachusetts House of Representatives. He was one of the Justices who tried the celebrated Mrs. Robinson poisoning case. He was a life-long member of Dr. Edward Everett Hale's Church, serving for many years on its Standing Committee, and taking a vital interest in the affairs of the congregation. Rev. Dr. Hale preached his funeral sermon."

(8) LUCY M. FARWELL b. Feb. 8, 1848.

(8) MARCIA W. FARWELL b. Jan. 17, 1851.

(8) NATHAN THOMAS FARWELL b. Sept. 12, 1853; d. Mch. 19, 1910, one of the most highly-respected citizens of Rockland, Me.; very successfully engaged in the banking business for many years; President of the North National Bank of Rockland; m. Dec. 25, 1877, Cora Maria Adams b. Union, Me., Apr. 12, 1854; a faithful member of the Congregational Church; a graduate of the Rockland High School; the daughter of William Adams and Elizabeth H. Leonard of Rockland, Me.

(9) ELIZABETH ADAMS FARWELL b. June 9, 1879.
(9) NATHAN ALLEN FARWELL b. Aug. 7, 1891; a student in Phillips Exeter, N. H., Academy; will enter Harvard University.

(8) TWINS, Jessie and Jennie Farwell, b. Feb., 1856, d. June, 1857.

(8) CHARLES G. FARWELL b. Aug. 12, 1858, d. July, 1861.

* * *

(7) ROBERT PERRY THOMAS b. May 20, 1818, d. Aug. 3, 1894; a very successful coal and lime dealer at Rockland, Me.; m. (1st) June 6, 1840, Charlotte Tolman who d. 1844; the daughter of Wm. Elliott Tolman and Sally Perry who resided at E. Thomaston, now Rockland, Me.; m. (2d) May 24, 1845, Lydia Maria Tolman b. Aug. 25, 1827, d. July 22, 1858; a sister of the first wife; m. (3) June 12, 1859, Martha Hannah Johnson b. Machiasport, Me., Aug. 17, 1837, d. Oct. 6, 1886; a member of the Baptist Church; the daughter of Hiram Johnson. Children of the first marriage:

----

(8) ELLEN THOMAS b. Nov. 1, 1840; resides Camden St., Rockland, Me.; m. Nov. 1, 1859, George Merrill Duncan, b. Lincolnville, Me., Dec. 23, 1834; Odd Fellow; caulker at Rockland, Me.; the son of Ingraham Duncan and Rebecca Norwood Perry of Rockland and Lincolnville, Me.

(9) HELEN DUNCAN b. Sept. 16, 1861, d. Jan. 26, 1909; m. Nov. 28, 1889, John E. Sullivan, a commercial traveler of Rockland, Me.; no children.

----

(8) SUSAN MARILLA THOMAS b. Apr. 1, 1842; resides 169 Scott Ave., Yonkers, N. Y.; unm.

Children of the second marriage of Robert P. Thomas, with Lydia M. Tolman.

----

(8) SARAH FRANCES THOMAS b. 1847, d. 1870; m. Richard Barney.

----

(8) CLARA ADA THOMAS b. Apr. 23, 1849, d. May 9, 1882; resided in Vinalhaven and Rockland, Me.; m. June 17, 1871, John Roscoe Frohock b. Northport, Me., Nov. 23, 1848; resides 63 Park St., Rockland, Me.; a successful dry goods merchant; Free Mason; Councilman 1897-1905; Ward Clerk, 1908-1910; the son of Joseph M. Frohock b. Searsport, Me., Jan. 18, 1814, and of Olive L. Calderwood b. Vinalhaven, Me., Apr. 5, 1822.

(9) NETTIE FREDERICA FROHOCK b. Aug. 28, 1872; resides Rockland, Me.; graduated from Rockland, Me., High School, 1892; m. Apr. 23, 1895, Frank Leander Weeks b. Rockland, Me.,

June 25, 1862; a successful dealer in crockery; Odd Fellow; the
son of Leander Weeks of Rockland and of Mary Jane Ross.

(10) DONALD ROSS WEEKS b. Apr. 14, 1896; student in Rockland, Me., High School.

(9) NINA EDWINA FROHOCK b. Rockland, Me., Dec. 13,
1875; resides 114 White St., Waverly, Mass.; graduated from
Rockland, Me., High School; graduated from Rockland, Me.,
Commercial College, 1894; m. Sept. 24, 1900, Morris Hazen
Goodwin b. Dover, N. H., Jan. 22, 1879; graduated from Rox-
bury, Mass., Grammar School; Clerk at Harvard Co-operative
Society, Harvard Square; the son of Samuel Hazen Goodwin
who now resides Lexington, Mass.; and of Helen Gowen.

(10) HAZEN WILBUR GOODWIN b. June 3, 1901.

(10) JOHN FROHOCK GOODWIN b. June 11, 1903.

(9) WILBUR CLYNTON FROHOCK m. Vinalhaven, Me., Feb.
13, 1879; carpet salesman at 117 Washington St., Boston, Mass.;
since his sixteenth year has resided in Boston, Mass.; Rockland,
Me., Grammar School; member of Royal Arcanum, No. 2;
Inspector in Ward No. 21, Boston, Mass., for one year; unm.

----

(8) LUCY EMMA THOMAS b. Mch. 2, 1853, d. July 29, 1892;
m. Dec. 25, 1876, Wilbur Fisk Coombs of Vinalhaven, Me., b.
Belfast, Me., Sept. 7, 1849; a hardware merchant; the children
reside at Vinalhaven, Me.

(9) ANNIE MERELIA COOMBS b. Sept. 24, 1879.

(9) RALPH BURK COOMBS b. Apr. 26, 1881.

(9) WILBUR FISKE COOMBS, J8., b. Oct. 31, 1886.

(9) MAYNARD THOMAS COOMBS b. Sept. 9, 1888.

Children of the third marriage of Robert P. Thomas, with
Martha H. Johnson.

(8) CHARLES SAWTELL THOMAS b. Mch. 13, 1860; sailor;
unm.; resides Rockland, Me.

(8) ISABEL THOMAS b. July 31, 1866; resides Camden St.,
Rockland, Me.; m. Oct. 15, 1890, Fred J. Hull of Rockland, Me.,
a salesman in a grocery story.

(9) WILLIAM T. HULL b. Apr. 10, 1892.

(9) HELEN S. HULL b. May 28, 1894.

(9) SARAH ELLA HULL b. July 22, 1896.

----

(8) ROBERT THOMAS b. Apr. 28, 1873; lime trimmer at Rockland, Me. Unm.

CHAPTER FIVE.

THE RECORDS OF CAPTAIN EPHRAIM PERRY (6).

* * *

(6) CAPTAIN EPHRAIM PERRY, the seventh child of Captain John Perry and Lucy Wooster, b. Dec. 21, 1788, d. at Rockland, Me., May 10, 1862; he was a very successful merchant mariner; Justice of the Peace, and Notary Public in 1844; he came to Rockland, Me., from the Fox Islands, Me., when a young man, and resided in that city all his life; m. Nov. 15, 1814, Nancy Crockett b. Sept. 10, 1789; the daughter of John Crockett; the granddaughter of Jonathan Crockett who came from Falmouth, now Portland, Me., and was one of the pioneer settlers of Rockland, Me.

* * *

(7) ANGELIA M. PERRY b. Mch. 20, 1815, d. Nov. 4, 1851; resided in Rockland, Me.; m. Oct. 13, 1834, as his first wife, Joseph Furbush, a very successful stove merchant of Rockland, Me.; born about 1813. He m. 2d Louise A. Wight.

(8) JOSEPH H. FURBUSH b. Aug. 9, 1833, d. Sept. 9, 1835.

(8) CAPTAIN MAURAN P. FURBUSH b. Dec. 18, 1837; lost in a snow storm, Dec. 10, 1864, in the schooner Lion, being wrecked on Simons' Point, Nahant, Mass.; his crew, five in number, perished with him; m. Sept. 12, 1862, Annie M. Parsons of Bangor, Me.; this family lived in Rockland, Me.

(9) MAURAN FURBUSH b. 1863.

(8) CAPTAIN FREDERICK FURBUSH b. Feb. 22, 1838, d. Oct. 26, 1863; died from yellow fever at New Orleans, La.; resided at Rockland, Me.; entered the U. S. Navy at Masters' Mate in 1862; promoted to Acting Ensign; unm.

(8) EMMA SOPHIA CROCKETT FURBUSH b. Sept. 22, 1842; d. Chicago, Ill.; resided in the West; m. Oct. 15, 1861, Alonzo Clifford Pease, b. Appleton, Me., Oct. 25, 1834; son of George Pease and Mary ——.

(9) FRED MAURICE PEASE b. May 25, 1865.

(8) RICHARD PITT FURBUSH b. 1849; he took the Perry name; a lime trimmer at Rockland, Me.; m. June 17, 1874, Dora Prescott of Rockland, Me.

(9) ANNIE DAGGETT PERRY b. Aug. 21, 1877.

(9) SWINEBURNE PITT PERRY b. Apr. 10, 1880.

(9) FRED MAURAN PERRY b. Apr. 6, 1886.

(9) MEDORA ANGELA PERRY b. Dec. 10, 1889.

(9) DOROTHY PERRY b. Apr. 6, 1892, d. May 11, 1897.

(9) HAROLD PRESCOTT PERRY b. May 9, 1894.

(9) DONALD PERRY b. Dec. 3, 1896.

(8) JOSEPH FURBUSH b. Oct. 15, 1851; d. Dec. 19, 1851.

* * *

(7) SOPHIA C. PERRY b. May 10, 1807, d. Jan. 10, 1886; lived Rockland; unm.

* * *

(7) CAPTAIN KNOTT CROCKETT PERRY b. Apr. 27, 1820, d. May 7, 1894; resided at Rockland, Me.; for fifteen years the very faithful Keeper of Indian Island Light, Rockland, Me.; a master mariner, and teacher of Navigation; m. July 18, 1843, Deborah L. Grant the daughter of Capt. John Grant and Hannah Lindsay; granddaughter of John Grant, who came from Cape Cod, Mass., to the Fox Islands, Me., in 1785.

(8) EPHRAIM PERRY b. May 22, 1844; Proprietor of Steam Dye and Cleansing House, Rockland, Mes.; m. Apr. 23, 1886, Helen Tripp of South Thomaston, Me.

(9) SUMNER C. PERRY b. June 26, 1888.

(9) DEBORAH L. PERRY b. Aug. 16, 1889.

(9) IRA L. PERRY b. Apr. 16, 1892.

(8) FREDERICK WILDER PERRY b. Apr. 1, 1849; sailor of Rockland, Me.; m. Sept. 5, 1888, Althea Batchelder; no children.

(8) REBECCA CROCKETT PERRY b. Sept. 2, 1851, d. Sept. 5, 1894; m. Dec. 12, 1880, John Colson, b. Rockland, Me., Sept. 6, 1846; a shoe dealer at Rockland, Me.; son of Thomas Colson and Sarah W. Tighe.

(9) EPHRAIM PERRY COLSON b. Sept. 11, 1882.

(9) FRED PERRY COLSON b. June 9, 1884.

(8) ELLEN ESTABROOK PERRY b. July 5, 1853; m. Dec. 13, 1875, John A. Keen, a grocer of Rockland, Me., b. Sept. 17, 1852; son of Dudley Tyler Keen and Rhoda Burrows.

(9) CHARLES SNOW KEEN b. Nov. 4, 1876.

(9) BESSIE BELLE KEEN b. Oct. 14, 1880.

(8) ANNIE SMITH PERRY b. Rockland, Me., Dec. 21, 1862; has lived in Maine towns, Vinalhaven, Belfast, Augusta, etc.; m. Jan. 16, 1882, Ira Tilson Lovejoy, b. Rockland, Me., Dec. 28,

1856, d. at Augusta, Me., Mch. 20, 1890; hotel proprietor; Odd Fellow; the son of Charles Crockett Lovejoy and Caroline Louise Keiser of Rockland, Me.

(9) ALICE LAURA LOVEJOY b. Rockland, Me., Mch. 23, 1882; Rockland High School, 1900; a very efficient accountant at Rockland.

(8) KNOTT C. PERRY, JR., b. Jan. 29, 1868.

* * *

(7) EPHRAIM MAURAN PERRY b. Feb. 2, 1823, d. Jan. 17, 1862; Cashier of Lime Rock National Bank, Rockland, Me.; unm.

* * *

(7) JOHN JARVIS PERRY b. Jan. 26, 1825; a very successful lime manufacturer, vessel owner and merchant at Rockland, Me.; also lived in N. Y. city; m. Aug. 4, 1852, Mary Frances Cowl of Brooklyn, N. Y.; b. N. Y. City Aug. 9, 1828, d. July 14, 1880; the daughter of Orrin Cowl, a merchant of New York City, and of Wealthy Roberts.

(8) JAMES HENRY COWL PERRY b. June 19 1853, d. Jan. 5, 1858.

(8) JARVIS CROCKETT PERRY b. July 4, 1856; resides Rockland, Me.; of Perry Brothers, manufacturers of lime and dealers in ship chandlery; m. Oct. 3, 1888, Edith Fances Hall, b. Oct. 22, 1859, daughter of Judge O. G. Hall of Rockland, now of Augusta, Me. A highly esteemed family of Rockland, Me.

(9) GWENDOLEN GRAY PERRY b. May 30, 1890.

(9) HELEN DAVENPORT PERRY b. June 24, 1891.

(9) JOHN JARVIS PERRY b. Oct. 21, 1893.

(9) EDITH ROSAMOND PERRY b. Feb. 5, 1895.

(9) STANDISH PERRY b. Dec. 2, 1898.

(8) ORRIN FRANCIS PERRY b. Oct. 10, 1858; a successful merchant of Rockland, Me.; now resides N. Y. City; m. Apr. 6, 1887, Marie Antoinnette Nash.

(9) ANNA LOUISE PERRY b. Mch. 5, 1888.

(9) GRACE ADELAIDE PERRY b. Mch. 2, 1890.

(9) ANTOINETTE FRANCES PERRY b. July 25, 1892.

(9) ORRIN FRANCIS PERRY b. Sept. 17, 1894.

(8) BENJAMIN COWL PERRY b. May 31, 1860; a successful merchant of Rockland, Me.; m. Feb. 18, 1881, Alfaretta Nash of Rockland, Me., b. July 4, 1861; of Capt. Ezekiel Nash and Catherine ———.

(9) MARY WEALTHY PERRY b. Sept. 12, 1882.

(9) MORRIS BENJAMIN PERRY b. Dec. 25, 1883.

(9) CLIFFORD ORRIN PERRY b. Aug. 7, 1885.

(9) HAZEL MAUD PERRY b. Mch. 30, 1887.

(9) MYRTLE LILIAS PERRY b. Jan. 18, 1889, d. Aug. 6, 1890.

(9) RAYMOND JARVIS PERRY b. Feb. 21, 1890, d. Aug. 18, 1890.

(9) ALFRED EZEKIEL PERRY b. Mch. 27, 1891, d. Oct. 13, 1891.

(9) ALFREDA CATHERINE PERRY b. Mch. 27, 1891.

(9) MARION EVELYN PERRY b. Aug. 9, 1892.

(9) KARL WILBUR PERRY b. Dec. 10, 1893.

(9) DORIS BRITT PERRY b. Dec. 10, 1894.

(9) BENJAMIN COWL PERRY, 2d, b. June 1, 1896.

(9) ALFARETTA ESTHER PERRY b. June 27, 1898.

* * *

(7) OLIVER A. PERRY b. Mch. 15, 1828, d. Apr. 9, 1829.

CHAPTER SIX.

THE RECORDS OF MARY PERRY (6) AND EZEKIEL
RAYMOND

* * *

(6) Mary Perry, the eighth child of Capt. John Perry and
Lucy Wooster, b. Jan. 27, 1791, d. Oct. 7, 1867; m. Ezekiel Ray-
mond of Vinalhaven, Me., b. Apr. 18, 1793, d. Northport, Me.,
Apr. 8, 1877.

* * *

(7) Abigail Raymond d. at Northport, Me.; m. Mch. 18,
1835, John Ames Dyer, who d. Nov. 8, 1877.

(8) Son b. Jan. 10, 1836, d. in infancy.

(8) Benjamin Franklin Dyer b. May 26, 1838, d. Northport, Me., Nov. 28, 1865.

(8) Mary Elizabeth Dyer b. June 1, 1841; deceased; m.
Elisha Calderwood.

(9) Nettie M. Calderwood m. Willis Witherspoon

(10) Nellie May Witherspoon; m. July, 1846, John
Crockett of N. Haven, Me.; the son of Deacon Samuel Crockett.

(11) Bernice Crockett b. Feb. 17, 1847; deceased.

(10) Leigh Floyd Witherspoon.

(8) Rebecca Ames Dyer b. Dec. 15, 1842; m. John Grant b.
Oct. 15,, 1842, d. Mch. 2, 1865.

(8) Hannah Dyer b. June 16, 1845; m. George Drinkwater
of Lincolnville, Me.; deceased.

(8) Jane Smith Dyer b. Aug. 12, 1847, d. Nov. 8, 1863.

(8) George W. Smith Dyer b. June 15, 1851; m. Dec. 29,
1875, Eldesta Ann Drinkwater of Northport, Me.; b. Jan. 19,
1853, d. Dec. 1, 1887.

(9) Cora Ellen Dyer b. Oct. 6, 1876; m. Aug., 1898, George
Sherman of Lincolnville, Me.

(10) Doris Eldesta Sherman b. May 1899.

(9) Mary Abbie Dyer b. Mch. 1879, d. (14 months).

(9) Walter Franklin Dyer b. Feb. 25, 1881.

(9) Charles Wentworth Dyer b. 1885, d. Northport, Me.,
Mch. 10, 1880.

* * *

(7) Asa Calderwood Raymond, the second child of Mary Perry and Ezekiel Raymond, b. Apr. 12, 1822, d. Vinalhaven, Me., July 25, 1897; m. Jan. 20, 1848,, Hannah Hudson Arey, who d. Mch. 6, 1890; the daughter of Ebenezer Arey and Azubia —— of Vinalhaven, Me.

(8) Ebenezer A. Raymond b. Nov. 1, 1848, d. Mch. 20, 1871.

(8) Washington Arey Raymond b. Jan. 4, 1850; deceased; m. Dec., 1874, at Brunswick, Me., Lillie Bell Sawyer.

(9) Howard Raymond b. Feb. 3, 1879.

(9) Mildred Belle Raymond.

(8) Irena Sylvester Raymond b. May 25, 1851; m. (1st) at North Haven, Me., Thomas Benjamin Brown, who was drowned 1898; the son of Thomas C. Brown and Susan —— of Barton's Island, Vinalhaven, Me. M. (2d) in Camden, Me., John P. Studley.

(9) Clarence Edwin Brown b. Apr. 16, 1874; m. Aug. 27, 1898, Mehitable Carter.

(10) Lysander Studley Brown b. Mt. Desert, Me., May 10, 1899.

(9) Henry Brown b. Nov. 9, 1877.

(9) Lester L. Brown b. Feb. 14, 1879.

Child of the 2d m. of Irena S. (Perry) Brown with J. P. Studley:

(9) Warren Studley b. Nov. 17, 1898.

(8) Martha Elva Raymond b. May 12, 1852, d. Sept. 10, 1873.

(8) Marianna Raymond b. May 1, 1854; m. Mch. 28, 1876, Charles Frederic Robbins of North Haven, Me., b. Nov., 1854; the son of William Robbins and Harriet Ames.

(9) Bertha Belle Robbins d. Aug. 19, 1889.

(9) Lyford Wilson Robbins b. Oct. 5, 1890.

(9) Clarabella Blanche Robbins b. Apr. 25, 1892.

(8) Luella Raymond b. Dec. 11, 1855, d. Sept. 2, 1884, at Vinalhaven, Me.; m. Henry Howard Brown of Barton's Island; no children.

(8) Sarah Evelyn Raymond b. Mch. 9 1858; m. Nocv. 27, 1891, Sidney Young; the son of Gideon Young of Lincolnville, Me.; no children.

(8) Dr. Hanson Llewellyn Raymond b. Apr. 14, 1859; a physician at Vinalhaven, Me.; m. Dec. 4, 1895, Bertha Healey b.

Apr. 18, 1868; the daughter of Chas. Healey and Maria Hall; no children.

(8) LUCRETIA BANKS RAYMOND b. July 11,1861; m. 1896 at W. Quincy, Mass.; Andrew Zastre; no children.

* * *

(7) ELONIA HURD RAYMOND, the third child of Ezekiel Raymond and Mary Perry, b. Dec. 24, 1824; resides Oldtown, Me.; m. Apr. 9, 1847, at Rockland, Me., Daniel Sawyer b. Saco, Me., Mch. 20, 1825, d. July 1, 1898; proprietor of a stove and tinware business. "As he was one of fourteen children in the home of a farmer of small means he left home when but fifteen years of age, walking from Saco to Portland, Maine, in quest of work. He learned the tinsmiths' trade at Bangor, Me., and then went to Rockland, remaining there some years. There he met his future wife, and they were married on a beautiful, summerlike day in April, and soon after their marriage they moved to Bangor, Me., where they lived for many years, their children all being born in that city. Just before the Civil War Daniel Sawyer became afflicted with the Western fever and went to Kansas and Indiana, where two of his brothers lived, to test the climate, etc. He enjoyed his visit, but he was entirely cured of his fever and never mentioned going West again. After the Civil War business was dull, and his health was not very good, and he bought a farm in Milo, Me., and moved his family there. But the experiences of four years convinced him that he was never intended for a farmer. So, as his brother, Thomas Sawyer, wished to retire from business at Oldtown, Me., an arrangement was made with him, so that he remained in Oldtown until his death; business was very good, and, in a moderate way, he prospered so that year by year he felt that he was laying up a little for his old age. He had many pleasant outings, one of these being to the World's Fair in Chicago, which he took with his youngest daughter. He and his wife were members of the Methodist Church, but he attended the Baptist Church for many years, and was a very efficient teacher in its Sunday School. He was buried in the Forest Hills Cemetery. He was the son of Andrew Sawyer and Elizabeth Brown."

(8) EMMA FRANCES SAWYER b. June 23, 1849, d. Mch. 30, 1887; m. Nov., 1871, Charles Dennis Gilbert b. Parkman, Me., May 1, 1849; tinsmith; no children.

(8) SARAH ELLA SAWYER b. Jan. 30, 1851, d. Apr. 1, 1875.

(8) ANNA MADELLE SAWYER b. Dec. 1, 1859; resides Old-town, Me.; m. May 22, 1880, Ethan Allen b. Lincoln Center, Me., Oct. 19, 1856; a plumber.

(9) Adopted son, Winnifred Raymond Allen b. Oct. 15, 1883.

* * *

(7) ROXANA DYER RAYMOND, the fourth child of Ezekiel Raymond and Mary Perry, b. Aug. 30, 1825; m. Dec. 17, 1851, Freeman Cobb Brown of Vinalhaven, Me.

(8) CHARLES ADELMAR BROWN b. Nov. 10, 1852; m. Jan. 1, 1875, at Marietta, Wis., Eleanor Celeste Metcalf.

(9) RUTH JANETTE BROWN b. Oct. 10, 1876.

(9) ROXANA DOROTHEA BROWN b. Mch. 11, 1880.

(9) RICHARD GARFIELD BROWN b. Apr. 29, 1882.

(9) FREDERIC CHARLES BROWN b. Aug. 30, 1887.

(8) DORA BROWN b. Oct. 6, 1854; m. at Marietta, Wis., May 1, 1874, Antone Topper.

(9) ADELINE TOPPER b. Feb. 11, 1876.

(9) ROXANA DELIA TOPPER b. Apr. 7, 1878.

(9) MELVINA AGNES TOPPER b. Apr. 1, 1880.

(9) MARY DORA TOPPER b. Nov. 3, 1882.

(9) FRANK TOPPER b. Mch. 4, 1885.

(9) MARTHA ANNIE TOPPER b. Mch. 10, 1887.

(9) CHARLES LEWIS TOPPER b. Jan. 8, 1890.

(9) ELLA MABELLE TOPPER b. Oct. 30, 1893.

(9) ALICE EDITH TOPPER b. Apr. 7, 1896.

(9) SUSIE PEARL TOPPER b. Jan. 22, 1898.

(8) FREEMAN LESLIE BROWN b. May 25, 1870; unm.

* * *

(7) DURA AMES RAYMOND b. Oct. 25, 1829; resides Vinal-haven, Me.; m. Aug. 9, 1851, Louisa J. Bennett.

(8) WILLIAM R. RAYMOND b. Jan. 14, 1858.

(8) EZEKIEL T. RAYMOND b. Oct. 26, 1861; m. July 25, 1886, Amanda Frances Arey.

(9) ANNIE ALMA RAYMOND b. Barton's Island, Me., Feb. 7, 1888.

(9) TWIN DAUGHTERS d. in infancy.

(9) FLORENCE MABEL RAYMOND b. Dec. 23, 1894.

(8) HERBERT FRANKLIN RAYMOND b. Mch. 13, 1866; m. Oct. 11, 1888, Maggie May Clark.

(9) SEWALL EUGENE RAYMOND b. Tenant's Harbor, Me.,
May 17, 1891, d. Sept. 21, 1891.

(9) NINA HAZEL RAYMOND b. Dec. 23, 1894.

(8) MARY EVELYN RAYMOND b. Aug. 14, 1871; m. Apr. 30,
1890, Christopher Holbrook.

(9) HAZEL LA VERNE HOLBROOK b. Apr. 23, 1893.

(9) EUGENE DURA HOLBROOK b. Aug. 1896.

(9) GRACE EVELYN HOLBROOK b. Mch. 12, 1898.

(8) CHARLES A. RAYMOND b. June 7, 1873.

(8) EUGENE C. RAYMOND b. Mch. 26, 1876.

(8) ADA FRANCES RAYMOND b. Dec. 27, 1878; m. Oct. 21,
1891, Anthony Levi b. Fayal, Western Islands, Apr. 1, 1849; no
children.

(8) NELLIE A. RAYMOND b. Feb. 13, 1885.

* * *

(7) MARTHA HARVEY RAYMOND b. Vinalhaven, Me., Feb. 20,
1833; R. F. D. No. 11, North Haven, Me.; has also lived in
Vinalhaven and Lincolnville, Me.; Vinalhaven schools; m. (1st)
Sept. 16, 1855, Tolman Burgess b. Matinicus Isle, Me., May 12,
1833, d. July 21, 1861; fisherman; a very brave soldier; enlisted
in the Civil War, May, 1861, Company C, 2d Maine Regiment;
shot at the first Bull Run battle; the son of Thomas Burgess and
Mary Young of Matinicus Isle, Me.; m. (2d) Oct. 12, 1893,
Albion Mills b. Vinalhaven, Me., Sept. 16, 1833; farmer; drafted
into the Union Army Sept. 22, 1864, and served in the 2d Maine
Regiment until the close of the Civil War; was in important battles; the son of Benjamin Mills b. Vinalhaven, Me., and of
Jerusha Dyer b. North Haven, Me.

(8) Child of the first marriage, James Leslie Burgess b. Belfast, Me., May 12, 1859; resides Hartford, Conn.; also lived at
Lincolnville, Me.; employed by an Ice Company; m. Dec. 3, 1888,
Hattie Fuller b. June 5, 1870; the daughter of Miles Fuller and
of Lydia Bartlett Heal, who resided at Linconville, Me., and are
deceased.

(9) LIONEL FULLER BURGESS b. Meriden, Conn., Sept. 27,
1889; graduated from Hartford, Conn., schools, 1910; resides 144
High St., Hartford, Conn.

(9) DE LONG BURGESS b. Hartford, Conn., Oct. 16, 1895.

* * *

(7) SALLIE VINAL RAYMOND b. Nov. 25, 1827, d. Aug. 29,
1885; buried in Walnut Hill Cemetery, Brookline, Mass.; resided

in Brookline, Mass., for many years; a noble and helpful woman; m. Nov. 29, 1849, Ira Albert Stubbs b. Bucksport, Me., Dec. 6, 1817, d. North Carver, Mass., June 11, 1888; a carpenter; a very industrious and faithful man.

(8) FREDDIE WARREN STUBBS b. 1853, d. at four months.

(8) JENNIE M. STUBBS b. Brookline, Mass., Mch. 17, 1857; resides 26 Bowker St., Brookline, Mass.; studied in Brookline, Mass., schools; a very faithful wife, mother and friend; m. June 2, 1879, Moses Franklin Kenrick b. Brookline, Mass., Jan. 17, 1857; schools of Brookline, Mass.; a man of sturdy qualities; very successful in the plumbing, heating and ventilating business; an Odd Fellow; the son of Alfred Kenrick who was born in Ireland, and of Sarah Burr Gleason, who was born in Dorchester, Mass.

(9) S. MAYBELLE KENRICK b. May 4, 1880; a faithful member of the Baptist Church; Brookline, Mass., schools; m. May 20, 1903, Arthur J. Macurdy; resides 19 Bradbury St., Alston, Mass.

(10) WARREN KENRICK MACURDY b. Mch. 16, 1904, d. (4 months).

(9) GRACE KENRICK b. Nov. 7, 1886; resides 202 Atlantic Ave., Swampscott, Mass.; Brookline, Mass., schools; member Baptist Church; m. Oct. 19, 1905, Fred Farr Woodell, b. Canada, Aug. 16, 1886; mechanic; of Prof. F. W. Woodell, Prof. of Singing in Boston, Mass., and of Emma Farr.

(9) ALFRED KENRICK b. Oct. 1, 1889; graduated from Brookline, Mass., High School, and entered Mass. Institute of Technology in 1908.

(9) CLARENCE VINAL KENRICK b. May 25, 1892; will graduate at·Brookline, Mass., High School, in 1911.

(8) CLARENCE PARKER STUBBS b. July 21, 1860, d. Oct. 21, 1865.

(8) HARRIET ALDANA STUBBS b. Apr. 16, 1862; resides 144 Main St., Rockland, Me.

(8) IDA MAY STUBBS b. Jan. 20, 1865; resides Vinalhaven, Me.; of great help in securing records for this book.

CHAPTER SEVEN

THE RECORDS OF MARGARET PERRY (6) AND
DAVID PHILBROOK

* * *

(6) MARGARET PERRY, the ninth child of Captain John Perry
and Lucy Wooster, b. Feb. 2, 1792, d. June 20, 1859; a woman
of the noblest character and dearly beloved by all her neighbors
and friends; m. Oct. 27, 1814, David Philbrook b. Nov. 30, 1789,
d. Islesboro, Me., Dec. 3, 1857; he had the sterling qualities which
have marked the Philbrook family through its long generations;
the son of Joseph Philbrook, who d. June 13, 1841; he lived on
Seven Hundred Acre Island, and was highway surveyor in 1794;
petitioner to the General Court in 1787; m. Polly Lassell of a very
brave and patriotic old family; "Joseph Philbrook was probably
the son of Jonathan Philbrook, who with his wife and nine children came from Greenland, N. H., to the Second Parish in
Georgetown, now West Bath, Me., in 1742. He built a house on
the Point, near where the mansion of Governor King stood. He
was the principal inhabitant of Georgetown, and, in May, 1753,
Jonathan Philbrook and forty-six others petitioned that they might
be set off into a separate, or second, parish. This petition was
granted, and the second Parish was organized Apr. 2, 1754, at the
house of Mr. Philbrook. He and his son, Lieutenant Jonathan
Philbrook, were two of the committee to procure a minister. In
1755 he and his sons built two coasting vessels, and I think they
may be called the pioneers in shipbuilding at Bath, Me. Jonathan
Philbrook, Jonathan, Jr., and Job Philbrook, were petitioners for
the new County of Lincoln, Me., in 1752. William Philbrook,
Joshua Philbrook, and Job Philbrook, were soldiers in the first
Company of the Second Parish of Georgetown, Me., in 1757. In
May, 1766, Job Philbrook was taken prisoner by the Indians, and
carried to Canada, but exchanged, and returned in October following. Of the sons of Jonathan Philbrook, William and Job,
and perhaps Joseph, moved to Islesboro, Me., at an early date."

See the very interesting History of Islesborough, Me., by Capt. John P. Farrow, 1893.

The children of David Philbrook and Margaret Perry:

* * *

(7) JANE PHILBROOK b. Mch. 23, 1815, d. June 12, 1817.

* * *

(7) MARY PHILBROOK b. Feb. 5, 1817, d. Oct. 25, 1820.

* * *

(7) JUDSON PHILBROOK b. Islesborough, Me., Apr. 8, 1820, lost at sea, Jan. 30, 1868; he was then in command of the Brig Julia Arey, and, during a fierce gale in the Gulf Stream, he was knocked overboard by some halyards parting, and a block striking him on the head; he went to Scotland as a sailor when he was but sixteen years of age; and he was Master of vessels for over twenty-five years, sailing to many Southern, West Indian, and European ports, and being widely recognized as one of the most competent and successful of Maine Captains; he safely crossed the ocean in the Brig O. C. Clary during the Civil War when the Atlantic was swarming with privateers; his wife and little son were with him on many such trips. M. Jan. 13, 1847 (Hist. Islesboro) Jane Farnsworth Pendleton b. Islesboro, Me., Jan. 10, 1827, d. Jan. 18, 1888 (61); a fine student in the Islesboro schools, and a woman of great courage and ability; a faithful member of the Islesboro Baptist Church; she was the daughter of John Pendleton, who inherited the old homestead of his father, and of his second wife, Betsy Farnsworth, who was a native of Waldoborough, Me. "John Pendleton was Deacon of the Church for many years, and died respected and regretted by all who knew him." He was the son of John Pendleton (2) and Peggy Young; and grandson of William Pendleton (1) b. Westerly, R. I., Feb. 11, 1727, and moved to Islesboro, Me., 1767-8.

———

(8) MARTHA JANE PHILBROOK b. Jan. 13, 1849; resides Islesboro, Me.; of great help in the writing of this family history; member of the Second Baptist Church, Islesboro, Me.; a fine student in the Islesboro, Me., schools; m. Dec. 29, 1873, Captain Delmar Gilkey b. Islesboro, Me., Oct. 8, 1847, d. Jan. 26, 1885; he followed the sea from sixteen to thirty-six years of age; sailing to Southern, West Indian, Mexican, and European ports, and

widely known for his efficient work; a Free Mason; the son of Avery Gilkey and Eliza Pendleton; grandson of Thomas Gilkey; and great-grandson of John Gilkey who settled at Islesboro, Me., prior to 1775; and of his wife, Sylvina Thomas. Children b. Islesboro, Me.

(9) AUGUSTUS PHILBROOK GILKEY b. Apr. 4, 1880, d. Nov. 1, 1907; he studied in Islesboro schools; and in Rockland, Me., Commercial School; graduating there 1892; he was a very successful hotel clerk in Boston for some time; then clerk and salesman in Islesboro, being everywhere liked for his faithfulness and industry; after his health failed he had the best of care, but died from Bright's Disease; a member of the First Baptist Church, Jacksonville, Florida; a young man of great promise.

(9) ADELMAR GILKEY b. Mch. 6, 1884; a fine student in the Grammar and High School, Malden, Mass.; graduated from Castine, Me., Normal School; a very successful teacher, and a young lady of marked ability.

(8) LUCY ANN PHILBROOK b. Mch. 7, 1842, d. Aug. 3, 1906; she was a most helpful member of the Baptist Church; m. Jan. 15, 1871, Capt. Winfield Scott Pendleton b. Islesboro, Me., Sept. 2, 1847; schools of Islesboro, Me.; a very successful sea Captain; then a merchant; Free Mason, member of the Blue Lodge, Royal Arch and Knights Templar; also an Odd Fellow; Representative to the Maine Legislature 1880 and in 1905. Senator, 1911. He was the son of Captain Mark Pendleton, Jr., and Eliza J. Coombs, daughter of Fields Coombs; grandson of Mark Pendleton and Lydia Ball; great-grandson of Samuel Pendleton and Bathsheba Dodge; great-great-grandson of Capt. Thomas Pendleton b. Westerly, R. I., and of Dorcas Dodge.

(9) WINFIELD SCOTT PENDLETON, JR., b. Apr. 15, 1872; office 77 South St., N. Y. City; ship chandler; schools of Islesboro, Me.; graduated from Castine, Me., Normal School and from Eastman's Business College, Poughkeepsie, N. Y.; m. June 3, 1903, Carolyn Lucy Johnson of Troy, N. Y.

(10) HARRISON LOCKWOOD PENDLETON b. June, 1904.

(9) DR. JUDSON PHILBROOK PENDLETON b. Sept. 25, 1873; 95 Sixth Ave., Brooklyn, N. Y.; graduated from Castine, Me., Normal School; a four years' course in East Maine Conference Seminary, Bucksport, Me.; graduating 1894; graduated from the College of Physicians and Surgeons, Columbia College; and at once

commenced his medical practice, in which he has been very successful. M. Elizabeth S. Emerson, who d. Jan. 29, 1911.

(9) LEWIS NEWTON PENDLETON b. Feb. 15, 1875; resides Islesboro, Me.; Islesboro schools; graduated from East Maine Conference Seminary; and from Eastman's Business College, Poughkeepsie, N. Y.; grocery merchant; m. Aug. 22, 1897, Dorothea Rodella Hatch b. Islesboro, Me., Aug. 7, 1873; Islesboro schools; daughter of Pyam Dodge Hatch and Myra Emma Pendleton of Islesboro, Me.; granddaughter of Deacon James Hatch b. Hanover, Mass., 1796; a resident of Islesboro, Me., for many years, Deacon of the Baptist Church; soldier of the 1812 War; m. Mary Townsend.

(9) ETHEL LUCINDA PENDLETON b. May 11, 1878, d. Mch. 10, 1881.

(9) MARK PENDLETON b. Feb. 12, 1883, d. Nov. 27, 1887.

(9) BOWDOIN NEALLY PENDLETON b. June 27, 1885; resides 95 6th Ave., Brooklyn, N. Y.; salesman for a lumber firm; has resided Brooklyn since Dec. 17, 1906; graduated from Coburn Classical School, Waterville, Me., June 16, 1905; member of the Baptist Church, Islesboro, Me.; member of Alpha Phi Society; a man of sterling qualities; unm.

(9) LESTER LEWIS PENDLETON b. Jan. 8, 1893.

----

(8) JUDSON AUGUSTUS PHILBROOK b. Sept. 10, 1845, lost at sea, Apr. 23, 1875; he was washed overboard from the schooner Mary Pendleton; he was but nineteen years old, but was the joy and light of his home; a young man of great integrity and promise.

* * *

(7) EMELINE PHILBROOK b. May 9, 1822, d. Aug. 22, 1825.

* * *

(7) ANGELIA FURBISH PHILBROOK b. Mch. 16, 1824, d. May 25, 1876; lived Camden and Seven Hundred Acre Island, Me.; she and her husband were faithful members of the Christian Band; m. Oct. 16, 1843, Aug. 30, 1844 (Hist. Islesboro, Me.) Capt. Elbridge Gerry Philbrook b. Islesboro, Maine, May 11, 1819, d. July 23, 1900; he was the son of Job Philbrook, Jr., and Sylvina Pendleton; grandson of Job Philbrook and Dolly Hinck-

ley; great-grandson of Jonathan Philbrook b. Greenland, N. H., and settled in Georgetown, Me.

---

(8) ELBRIDGE MARION PHILBROOK b. Oct. 29, 1844, d. May 5, 1872; sailor; m. Dec. 25, 1864, Georgia Littlejohn of Cape Elizabeth, Me., the daughter of Chas. Littlejohn and Georgia——.
(9) BRADFORD MARION PHILBROOK b. Mch. 25, 1868.

---

(8) FLORENCE ANGELIA PHILBROOK b. Islesboro, Me., July 23, 1846; has lived in Islesboro; Boston, Mass.; N. Y. City; Castine, Me.; m. Oct. 3, 1868, Luther Coombs Farnsworth, b. Islesboro, Me., Aug. 26, 1844; member of the Baptist Church; graduated from East Maine Conference Seminary, Bucksport, Me.; son of Arthur Farnsworth and Louisa Coombs.
(10) MYRON ARTHUR FARNSWORTH b. May 11, 1870; resides 15 Walk Hill St., Forest Hills, Mass.; has also lived in Medford and Upton, Mass.; studied in the schools of Islesboro, Me., and Boston, Mass.; carpenter and steward; an Odd Fellow and Free Mason; m. Nov. 6, 1892, Leila Rosa Haynes of Islesboro, Me., b. Oct. 8, 1872; daughter of Solomon W. Haynes and Abby Van Amburg; granddaughter of Samuel Haynes and Rosanna Marshall.
· (11) WALTER MYRON FARNSWORTH b. Aug. 25, 1894.
(11) EARLE GRANVILLE FARNSWORTH b. Mch. 17, 1896.
(11) MILDRED EVANGELINE FARNSWORTH.
(11) JERRY BERTRAM FARNSWORTH.
(10) JAMES MELVIN FARNSWORTH b. July 29, 1872; graduated from the East Maine Conference Seminary; cutter in a shoe shop; attends the Baptist Church; m. Oct. 17, 1893, Margaret Armena Hamon of Oxford, Nova Scotia; daughter of John Hamon, 515 Quincy St., Brockton, Mass.
(11) LEILA FLORENCE FARNSWORTH b. Aug. 13, 1894.
(11) PERCY MELVIN FARNSWORTH b. Aug. 26, 1896.
(11) ELMER HOUSTON FARNSWORTH b. Jan. 15, 1898.
(11) HERBERT ROY FARNSWORTH b. Feb. 25, 1900.
(10) NAHUM COOMBS FARNSWORTH b. Oct. 26, 1874; 44 Pearl St., Brockton, Mass.; resided in Islesboro, Me., fifteen years; followed the sea until 1895; lived in Brockton, Mass., ever since; employed in a Box Toe Manufactory; member of the First Congregational Church, Brockton, Mass.; Islesboro, Me., schools. M. Lula Etheline Hatch b. Sept. 21, 1876; daughter of George W.

Hatch who m. Oct. 31, 1861, Eliza Gilkey; parents live Brockton, Mass.

(11) PEARL WESLEY FARNSWORTH b. Apr. 6, 1900.

(11) GRACIE BURNETT FARNSWORTH b. Dec. 28, 1901.

(11) RALPH EMERSON FARNSWORTH b. Dec. 18, 1904.

(11) ROLAND FARNSWORTH still born Feb. 8, 1899.

(10) ANNIE LOUISE FARNSWORTH b. Aug. 26, 1882; graduated from Castine, Me., Normal School; teacher.

(10) LEILA FLORENCE FARNSWORTH b. May 5, 1885; resides Islesboro, Me., with her parents; graduated from Islesboro, Me., High School.

(10) EUGENE LUTHER FARNSWORTH b. July 30, 1887; resides Oldtown, Me.

(9) JUDSON PHILBROOK b. June 9, 1848; farmer at Union and Appleton, Me.; m. 1874 Lizzie McKenney of Appleton, Me.; b. Lincolnville, Me.

(10) HOLLIS EVERETT PHILBROOK b. Nov. 23, 1875.

(10) EMMA GRACE PHILBROOK b. Feb. 24, 1878.

(10) EUGENE LYMAN PHILBROOK b. Oct. 7, 1879.

(10) MELVIN PHILBROOK b. Sept. 1, 1881.

(10) ARTHUR LYMAN PHILBROOK b. July 29, 1888.

(9) HOLLIS COX PHILBROOK b. July 29, 1850, d. 1888.

(9) GEORGE EVERETT PHILBROOK b. Sept. 21, 1852, d. 1895; m. Mary ——— of Liverpool, England.

(9) MELVIN WISWELL PHILBROOK b. Nov. 18, 1854, d. 1872.

(9) MARY LAVERNE PHILBROOK b. Nov. 19, 1854, d. Sept. 20, 1873.

* * *

(7) ORINDA PHILBROOK b. Islesboro, Me., May 1, 1827; resides Belfast, Me.; studied in Islesboro, Me., schools; lived Islesboro, Lincolnville, Northport, and Belfast, Me.; member of the Baptist Church; m. (1st) May 26, 1846, Samuel M. Haskell b. Wilton, Me., Apr. 2, 1816, d. Aug. 6, 1849; seaman; m. (2d) Mch. 27, 1851, David Williams b. Lincolnville, Me., Jan. 22, 1811, d. Feb. 9, 1891; seaman and farmer; son of David Williams and Nancy Mariner, who lived in Bath and Lincolnville, Me. Children of the second marriage.

(8) MAURICE WILLIAMS b. June 26, 1852, d. Northport, Me., Nov. 6, 1890; Islesboro, Me., schools; seaman and farmer.

(8) Willis Williams b. Mch. 11, 1855; resides Camden, Me.; yachtsman and builder; he and his wife members of the Baptist Church, Camden, Me.; m. Oct. 22, 1889, Mrs. Lelia F. (Perry) Champlin b. June 30, 1851.

(9) David Edward Williams b. Oct. 20, 1891, d. May 30, 1893.

---

(8) Edward Williams b. Apr. 9, 1857; now resides East Jaffrey, N. H.; lived in Boston, Mass., 1885; S. Framingham, Mass., 1898; Peterboro, N. H., 1906; schools of Islesboro, Me.; member of A. O. U. W.; chair maker and carpenter; m. Aug. 6, 1882, Ellen Frances Crowe of E. Jaffrey, N. H., b. Feb. 12, 1855; no children.

---

(8) Lucy Ann Williams b. May 10, 1859, d. Northport, Me., May 8, 1907; m. Dec. 24, 1882, Charles Drinkwater, b. Jan. 27, 1858; no children.

---

(8) Margaret Jane Williams b. Islesboro, Me., Aug. 12, 1861; resides 64 Church St., Belfast, Me.; Islesboro schools; lived in Islesboro till 1878; Lincolnville, Me., until 1885; Northport, Me., until 1905; Worcester and Roxbury, Mass.; member of the Adventist Church, Worcester, Mass.

---

(8) Ineztella, writes her name Inez T., Williams b. Mch. 7, 1866; resides Lincolnville, Me.; lived in Islesboro, Me., until 1879; Lincolnville until 1886; Northport until 1909; m. Sept. 14, 1891, William Henry Rossiter b. North Haven, Me., May 23, 1864; yachtsman; son of John T. Rossiter and Rebecca Ames of N. Haven and Northport, Me.

(9) Elmer Willliams Rossiter b. Dec. 18, 1894; Northport and Lincolnville, Me., schools.   . .

(9) Hugh Donald Rossiter b. May 22, 1897.

(9) Bernice Orinda Rossiter b. Feb. 20, 1901.

(9) Willis Edward Rossiter b. Nov. 28, 1902.

* * *

(7) Felix Philbrook b. Aug. 2, 1828, d. Sept. 15, 1837.

* * *

(7) Elonia Philbrook b. Islesboro, Me., June 21, 1831; resides Islesboro, Mt.; has lived in Islesboro and Rockland, Me.;

Islesboro, Me., schools; m. Nov. 22, 1851, Capt. John Pendleton
Farrow b. Islesboro, Me., Oct. 30, 1828, d. Oct. 4, 1902; steam-
boat Captain, Master Mariner; farmer; author of the excellent
"History of Islesborough, Me.;" studied in Chelsea, Mass.,
schools; the son of John Farrow and Harriet Pendleton, who
lived in Islesboro, Me., and in Boston, Mass.

---

(8) CAPT. JOHN OSCAR FARROW b. Oct. 1, 1852; resides 15
Pleasant street, Saco, Me.; Islesboro, Me., schools; has lived
Islesboro, Rockland, Me., 1906-1907; Saco, Me., 1908-1909; Master Mariner and Yacht Capt.; attends Free Baptist Church; member of Island Lodge, Free Masons, Islesboro, Me.; and of Lone
Star Chapter, Eastern Star; m. Dec. 31, 1876, Emily Ann Hatch
b. Islesboro, Me., Apr. 18, 1859; Islesboro, Me., schools; daughter of William E. Hatch and Emily Farrow of Islesboro, Me.

(9) COCHIE ELONA FARROW b. Apr. 5, 1878, d. from con-
sumption at Southern Pines, North Carolina, Jan. 1, 1906; studied
in Castine, Me., Normal School; a very successful teacher at
Islesboro, Me.; m. Sept. 14, 1903, Llewellyn T. Fairchild.

(9) CAPT. WILLIAM ELLIS FARROW b. Isleboro, Me., July 28,
1879; resides North Islesboro, Me.; studied in the Islesboro
schools; has been a very successful Master Mariner for several
years; sailing to Southern, and other, ports; is now in command
of the fine, four-masted schooner, Florence Howard, owned by
the Atlantic Shipping Company of Stonington, Conn.; a young
man of great ability and sturdy qualities; member of the Eastern
Star Masonic Lodge; m. June 27, 1901, Josie Emma Fairfield b.
July 20, 1879; studied in the Islesboro schools; the daughter of
Andrew Pendleton Fairfield and Joanna Persley Veazie, both of
Islesboro, Me.; deceased; granddaughter of Stephen Fairfield and
his second wife, Helen Pendleton.

(10) EMILY LUCRETIA FARROW b. Aug. 27, 1903.

(9) JOHN MALCOLM FARROW b. Islesboro, Me., May 13,
1885; resides Owl's Head, Me.; has also lived in Rockland and
Biddeford, Me.; studied in Islesboro schools; and in Rockland,
Me., Commercial College; was clerk in a tea store; also for a
Beef Company; is now a very successful engineer; m. Mch. 14,
1908, Ethel Florence Tolman of Owl's Head, Me., b. S. Thomas-
ton, Me., June 10, 1885; daughter of Ezekiel Ames Tolman and
Mary Lenora Whitelur.

(8) Capt. Herman Malcolm Farrow b. Mch. 31, 1865; resides Islesboro, Me., farmer; until twenty-one years of age; then an engineer and Mate; Master Mariner for over eighteen years; a Free Mason; m. Feb. 12, 1889, Laura Emma Grindle b. Islesboro, Me., Nov. 3, 1867; Islesboro, Me., schools; member of the First Baptist Church, Islesboro, Me.; daughter of Captain James F. Grindle and Theresa P. Rose; ganddaughter of Francis Grindle, Esq., and of his second wife, Mrs. Eliza (Harlow) Pendleton.

(9) Infant Son d. Feb. 14, 1898.

(9) Henry Grindle Farrow b. Islesboro, Me., Feb. 7, 1904.

(9) Herman Frank Pendleton Farrow b. Waltham, Mass., Jan. 1, 1908.

(8) Hattie Ernestine Farrow b. May 20, 1872; resides 29 Adamantan Ave., Rockland, Me., studied in Islesboro, Me., schools; m. Nov., 1899, Manley Warren Hart of Lincolnville, Me.; grocer.

(9) Marjorie Ernestine Hart b. May 7, 1901, d. from spinal meningitis, Feb. 7, 1906.

(9) Herman Manley Hart b. Jan. 31, 1904.

* * *

(7) David Philbrook, Jr., b. Jan. 27, 1834, d. New Haven, Conn., June 13, 1862; enlisted in the Civil War, 1861; wounded at the battle of Fair Oaks, May 31, 1862; m. June, 1857, Sarah Pendleton Warren, b. Apr. 23, 1834, d. Feb. 24, 1859 (24); daughter of Isaac Warren and Sally Pendleton; granddaughter of George Warren and Lydia Hatch; great-granddaughter of Samuel Warren, Senior.

(8) Alfred Philbrook b. June 10, 1856, d. Feb. 24, 1859.

* * *

(7) Oliver Philbrook b. Apr. 24, 1836; d. Jan. 1, 1842.

* * *

(7) Allison Philbrook b. July 23, 1839, d. Oct. 6, 1841.

CHAPTER EIGHT.

THE RECORDS OF CAPTAIN ROBERT PERRY (6).

* * *

(6) CAPTAIN ROBERT PERRY, the tenth child of John Perry and Lucy Wooster, b. Apr. 21, 1794, d. from yellow fever, in New York City, Jan. 31, 1851; m. (1st) Aug. 2, 1821, Dollie Spear b. Mch. 12, 1803, d. Aug. 2, 1824; daughter of Isaac Spear; granddaughter of Jonathan Spear who came from Braintree, Mass., to Thomaston, Me. M. (2d) Sept. 2, 1827, Melicent Eaton b. Jan. 7, 1804, d. Sept. 5, 1878; the daughter of Samuel Eaton and Mary Perry. Of 1st m.:

* * *

(7) HARRIET PERRY b. May 5, 1822, d. July 14, 1829.

* * *

(7) DOLLIE PERRY b. Apr. 30, 1824; resided 10 Locust St., Rockland, Me.; m. June 26, 1842, Patrick W. Walsh of Rockland, Me., b. East Boston, Mass. Aug. 12, 1816, d. Oct. 28, 1878; merchant, and lime manufacturer; the son of William Walsh, 2d, and Nancy Watson; grandson of William Walsh.

(8) HARVEY S. WALSH b. Nov. 17, 1845; resided Boston, Mass.; mariner; enlisted in the U. S. Navy, 1863; m. Emeline B. Hallock.

(9) ELIZABETH A. WALSH b. Aug. 24, 1872; m. Dec. 17, 1891, Albert E. Simpson, who d. 1900; electrical worker.

(10) JOHN D. SIMPSON b. June 16, 1895.

(9) HARRY C. WALSH b. Oct. 24, 1876, d. Aug. 17, 1898.

(9) RALPH O. WALSH b. Mch. 25, 1884, d. June 19, 1893.

(8) PATRICK J. WALSH b. about 1847; lived Rockland, Me.; entered U. S. Navy.

(8) FRANK WALSH b. about 1849.

Children of the second marriage of Robert Perry, with Melicent Eaton.

* * *

(7) EDWARD C. PERRY b. Jan. 15, 1829, d. May 3, 1832.

* * *

(7) JASPER PERRY b. Dec. 10, 1830, d. Sept. 11, 1831.

* * *

(7) GEORGE SPEARE PERRY b. Jan. 11, 1832; teacher; resided for some time at 290 Sackett St., Brooklyn, N. Y.; sailmaker; m. Jan. 25, 1866, Sarah E. Ash of Brooklyn, N. Y.

(8) SUSIE PERRY b. Nov. 29, 1867; m. Apr. 27, 1887, Robert Burns Cleland of Brooklyn, N. Y.

(9) ALICE FOREST CLELAND b. Feb. 28, 1890.

(8) ANNIE LOUISE PERRY b. Mch., 1869, d. Mch., 1869.

(8) MELICENT PERRY b. Feb. 5, 1878.

* * *

(7) CHARLES C. PERRY b. Apr. 24, 1833, d. at Rockland, Me., June 25, 1895; mariner; sailmaker; a brave soldier in the Civil War, in the fourth Maine Regiment.

* * *

(7) MARY E. PERRY b. Jan. 23, 1836; unm.

* * *

(7) ROBERT FRANK PERRY b. Oct. 28, 1837; sailmaker; resided on the old Rockland, Me., homestead; 558 Main St., Rockland, Me. M. Feb. 2, 1862, Eliza J. Aldrich.

* * *

(7) ORRIN C. PERRY b. Apr. 29, 1839; sailmaker at Thomaston, Me.; m. Oct. 18, 1873, Ella R. Swett b. Thomaston, Me., May 23, 1853; the daughter of Lorenzo Swett and Celestia Case.

(8) ROBERT L. PERRY b. May 10, 1877.

(8) LIZZIE C. PERRY b. June 30, 1880.

(8) BELLE S. PERRY b. Feb. 3, 1889.

(8) NELLIE PERRY b. Sept. 23, 1892.

* * *

(7) EDWARD C. PERRY b. Oct. 28, 1842, d. in youth.

* * *

(7) LUCY ANN PERRY b. Mch. 25, 1847; unm.

CHAPTER NINE.

THE RECORDS OF ELONIA PERRY (6) AND MOSES H. HEARD.

* * *

(6) ELONIA PERRY, the eleventh child of Captain John Perry and Lucy Wooster, b. Feb. 7 (15), 1796, d. Jan. 27, 1857 (61); m. Nov. 17, 1817, Moses H. Heard who d. Mch. 28, 1877 (87-10); "his grandfather Heard came from England with a brother; we do not know where this brother settled."

* * *

(7) NANCY PERRY HEARD b. Sept. 4, 1818, d. July 22, 1842; m. Sept., 1840, Alfed Haskell.

* * *

(7) MARY RAYMOND HEARD b. Mch. 25, 1820, d. Oct. 18, 1861.

* * *

(7) OLIVER HEARD b. Dec. 25, 1821; "he left home some fifty-five years ago, and, after drifting to almost every port of the world, at length brought up in the Sailors' Snug Harbor, N. Y."

* * *

(7) MARGARET MARANDA HEARD b. May 25, 1829; m. May 22, 1850, Captain Joshua Clark.

(8) KATE ELVA CLARK b. Oct. 2, 1852; m. June 4, 1870, Henry R. Heard; resides at Ash Point, Me.

(9) ETTA LENORE HEARD b. May 13, 1871; m. May 21, 1890, Mark L. Tripp.

(8) GEORGIE PERRY CLARK b. May 20, 1854; d. July 4, 1885; m. Apr. 5, 1876, John E. Hatch.

(9) EDWIN PERRY HATCH b. Apr. 20, 1878.

(9) FLORENCE BELLE HATCH b. July 23, 1879.

(8) JULIA BELLE CLARK b. S. Thomaston, Me., May 17, 1856; resides Rockland, Me.; member of the Baptist Church; m. Apr. 23, 1873, Edgar Johnson Southard of Winterport, Me.; b. Brooksville, Me., Oct. 10, 1852; contractor, builder, and mason;

the son of Samuel Newell Southard and Betsy Johnson Grindle of Rockport, Me., and of Stoneham, Mass.

(9) WILLIAM HENRY SOUTHARD b. July 31, 1874, d. Dec. 22, 1891.

(9) JOSHUA NEWELL SOUTHARD b. July 11, 1880; graduated from Rockland, Me., Commercial College, 1899.

(9) BESSIE CLARK SOUTHARD b. Oct 8, 1889; graduated from Rockland, Me., High School, 1909.

* * *

(7) CAROLINE M. HEARD b. July 24, 1831; resided Thomaston, Me.; m. Vespasian F. Hinckley, who d. Apr. 24, 1866.

(8) FRED T. HINCKLEY b. Sept. 17, 1855.

(8) HELEN F. HINCKLEY b. Sept. 20, 1860.

* * *

(7) JULIA B. HEARD b. Sept. 25, 1833; resides Caribou, Me.; m. Dec. 5, 1852, Charles W. Rackliffe.

(8) IDA RACKLIFFE b. Sept. 13, 1853, d. June 28, 1854.

(8) ELONIA T. RACKLIFFE b. Sept. 5, 1859.

(8) OLIVE N. RACKLIFFE b. Apr. 23, 1861.

(8) JOSHUA J. C. RACKLIFFE b. Mch. 6, 1864.

CHAPTER TEN.

THE RECORDS OF REBECCA PERRY (6) AND DANIEL THOMAS AND SAMUEL MOODY.

* * *

(6) REBECCA PERRY, the thirteenth child of Captain John Perry and Lucy Wooster, b. June 22, 1801, d. Aug. 22, 1870; m. (1st) Sept. 2, 1820, Daniel Thomas, who d. June, 1837; m. (2d) Aug., 1844, Samuel Moody, and resided at Belmont, Me.; no children of the second marriage.

* * *

(7) REBECCA THOMAS b. Oct. 14, 1821, d. 1840 (19).

* * *

(7) ABIGAIL THOMAS b. June 20, 1823, d. 1909, at Belfast, Me.; m. Daniel Thomas, the son of Tilden Thomas, who was b. Feb. 22, 1786; m. Charity Sylvester and lived at Northport, Me.

(8) GEORGE THOMAS. (8) ELBRIDGE THOMAS. (8) CHARITY THOMAS. (8) FLORA THOMAS m. Mr. Gilman. (8) DAUGHTER lived in Belfast, Me., for a time.

* * *

(7) DANIEL W. THOMAS b. Feb. 14, 1828; was for some time at Sailors' Snug Harbor, New Brighton, Staten Island, N. Y.; m. Aug. 2, 1854, Roanna Clementine Sherman of Islesboro, Me., b. Dec. 4, 1834.

(8) CAPTAIN CHESTER CLEVELAND THOMAS b. Islesboro, Me., May 27, 1857, d. in N. Y. City, Feb. 7, 1889. A very brave and enterprising Captain, commanding the three-masted schooner, Anna C. Pendleton. "He arrived in N. Y. City on the night of Feb. 17, 1899, after just outliving a terrible gale and snow storm. He had to leave his vessel down at Staten Island on account of the ice, and went up to the City on a tug boat. He went to his broker's and drew out $200.00. Being very tired, and having had no sleep for three nights, he went to a hotel instead of returning to his vessel. He went to his room about eight o'clock, and when the bell boy went his rounds at eleven o'clock he noticed the smell

of gas coming from Captain Thomas' room. Men quickly obtained keys and entered the room, but Captain Thomas was dead.
He had been robbed, and the general opinion is that he had been
suffocated with chloroform, and the gas turned on for a blind. A
physician was at once summoned, but he could do nothing. It is
supposed the robbers left the window open so as to disclose the
escaping gas, and that they did not intend to kill him. He was a
very smart, capable young man." M. Jan. 29, 1882, Rosalind
Parker of Islesboro, Me.; b. Sept. 10, 1861 ; a member of the Free
Baptist Church. (She m. (2d) Dec. 29, 1905, Robert Pendleton
Coombs b. Islesboro, Me., May 3, 1860; carpenter and mason;
the son of Martin Stone Coombs and Catherine M. Pendleton.)

(9) BERNICE ROSALIND THOMAS b. Mch. 29, 1885 ; resides 18
Lawrence St., Waltham, Mass.; graduated from Waltham, Mass.,
High School; m. Oct. 9, 1908, Harold Bertram Johnson b.
Waltham, Mass., Jan. 14, 1886; commercial traveler.

(10) THELMA JOHNSON b. July 5, 1909.

(9) ADRIANA BUNKER THOMAS b. Jan. 12, 1889; resides 189
Main St., Andover, Mass.; Governess.

(9) HARRISON CLEVELAND THOMAS b. Mch. 17, 1891; graduated from Rockland, Me., Commercial College; 58 Broadway,
Rockland, Me.

(9) CURTIS STANWOOD THOMAS b. May 12, 1895; graduated
from Islesboro, Me., Grammar School, 1908; mail carrier.

(8) CORA ANNA THOMAS b. Sept. 9, 1861 ; m. July 7, 1890,
Preston I. Merrill, who has charge of a Teachers' Agency, Tremont Temple, Boston, Mass.

(9) ALICE CHESLEY MERRILL b. Aug. 21, 1891.

(9) SEYMOUR MERRILL b. Aug. 5, 1898.

(8) ERNEST MORTIMER THOMAS b. Jan. 27, 1864, d. 1906; m.
Jan. 27, 1891, Margaret Babbidge, who resides Dark Harbor, Me.

(9) Two children died in infancy.

(8) OSMOND WELLINGTON THOMAS b. Oct. 13, 1872; resides
Dark Harbor, Me.

* * *

(7) IDDO THOMAS b. Oct. 3, 1833, d. "about 1878."

* * *

(7) CYNTHIA WEST THOMAS b. Seven Hundred Acre Island,
Islesboro, Me., July 23, 1836; resides Centre Belmont, Me.; m.
July 30, 1854, Hiram Brewster, 3d, b. Belmont, Me., May 14,

1832; ship carpenter and farmer; the son of Joseph Brewster of Belmont, Me., and of Abigail Tilden of Belmont, Me.

(8) CHARLES MAY BREWSTER b. Belmont, Me., Oct. 20, 1855; fireman, carpenter and farmer; Free Mason; Odd Fellow; m. Apr. 27, 1898, Sadie E. Crowell, b. Yarmouth, Nova Scotia. No childen.

(8) FRANK PERRY BREWSTER b. Sept. 5, 1858; ship carpenter; m. July 1, 1886, Flora E. Packard of Searsmont, Me.; the daughter of Edward Packard and Amanda Mahoney.

(8) MILES STANDISH BREWSTER b. Belmont, Me., Mch. 14, 1860; shoemaker and farmer; Odd Fellow; m. Dec. 27, 1882, Annie J. Thomas b. Belmont, Me., June 4, 1863; the daughter of Timothy D. Thomas and Nancy J. Wyman of Belmont and Searsport, Me.

(9) CARL STANDISH BREWSTER b. Apr. 29, 1896.

INDEX TO PERRY GENEALOGY

INDEX TO PERRY HISTORY

OTHER NAMES THAN PERRY

false118   OUR PERRY FAMILY IN MAINE

Chas. W.,	Page 23	HALL	
Dr. Edward T.,	Page 38	Aldeb T.,	Page 53
Ellery A.,	Page 23	Clara,	Page 22
Hattie,	Page 90	Edith,	Page 84
Henry M.,	Page 26	Maria,	Page 88
Mary A.,	Page 59	Judge O. G.,	Page 84
Miles,	Page 90	HALLOCK, Emeline B.,	Page 101
Rufus W.,	Page 23	HAM, Mrs. Sarah F.,	Page 71
FURBUSH		HAMON	
Emma S. C.,	Page 82	John,	Page 97
Capt. Frederick,	Page 82	Margaret,	Page 97
Joseph,	Pages 82, 83	HANLEY	
Joseph H.,	Page 82	Frances L.,	Page 68
Joseph N.,	Page 82	Jeremiah,	Page 68
Mauran,	Page 82	Thomas,	Page 68
Mauran P.,	Page 82	HANCOCK, John,	Pages 7, 10
Richard P.,	Page 82	HARRINGTON, Elizabeth,	Page 5
GARY, Wm.,	Page 6	HARRIS, John O.,	Page 26
GILBERT, Chas. D.,	Page 88	HASBROOK	
GILES		Chas. E.,	Page 25
Edwin L.,	Page 18	Ethelberta,	Page 25
Lydia A.,	Page 20	HASKELL	
Wm.,	Page 18	Alfred,	Page 103
GILKEY		Edith G.,	Page 32
Adelmar,	Page 94	H. G. O.,	Page 32
Augustus P.,	Page 94	HASTINGS	
Capt. Delmar,	Page 93	Bela S.,	Pages 26, 28
Eliza,	Page 97	Bertha G.,	Page 28
John,	Page 94	Edmond B.,	Page 74
GILL, Edward N.,	Page 21	Erwin,	Page 74
GILSON, Bessie N.,	Page 74	HATCH	
GRAFFAM, Elithea,	Page 38	Dorothea R.,	Page 95
GRANT, Deborah E.,	Page 83	Edward P.,	Page 99
John,	Page 83	Florence B.,	Page 103
GRINDLE		George W.,	Page 96
Betsey J.,	Page 104	Hannah A.,	Page 76
Frances,	Page 100	James,	Page 95
James F.,	Page 100	John E.,	Page 103
GOODWIN		Julia A.,	Page 76
Ellen L.,	Page 72	Lucy H.,	Page 75
Hazen W.,	Page 81	Lulu A.,	Page 75
John F.,	Page 81	Lydia,	Page 100
Susie H.,	Page 81	Pyam D.,	Page 95
HADWEN		Stephen,	Page 75
Annie C. (Ray),	Page 56	Hon. Stephen N.,	Page 75
HAHN		Wm. E.,	Page 70
Jacob,	Page 39	HAYES	
Dr. Wm. H.,	Page 39	Mildred,	Page 70
HALE, Dr. Edward E.,	Page 78	Leila R.,	Page 97

126 OUR PERRY FAMILY IN MAINE

Eva, Page 22
Henry F., Page 18
Inez, Page 98
Isaiah, Page 17
Jerry P., Page 18
John F., Page 6
Levi D., Page 17
Lillie M., Page 18
Louisa J., Page 18
Lucy A., Page 98
Marcy, Page 5
Margaret J., Page 98
Maurice, Page 97
Rose E., Page 18
Willis, Page 98
WILLISTON, Gertrude E., Page 32
WINSLOW
Allen P., Page 41
Arthur K., Page 42
Burton H., Page 41
Clara E., Page 42
Edward D., Pages 41, 42
Nelly P., Page 42
Winthrop, Page 42
WITHERSPOON
Leigh F., Page 86
Nellie M., Page 86
Willis, Page 86
WITHINGTON
Ephraim, Page 69
Julia, Page 69
WOOD
Berthia, Pages 4, 5
Nicholas, Page 5
WOODBURY
Chas. F., Page 73
Maj. Chas. H. B., Page 73
Pauline Page 73
Wm. C. Page 73
WOODELL
Fred F., Page 91
F. W., Page 91
WORRALL
Matilda W., Page 72
Nathan H., Page 72
WOOSTER
David, Page 12
Edward, Page 12
Joseph, Page 12
Lucy, Pages 12, 15, 66, 82, 86, 92,

101, 105
Lydia, Page 12
Margaret, Page 12
WYLIE
Capt. Almon L., Page 20
Alonzo P., Page 23
Annie M., Page 21
Arthur W. P., Page 29
Chas., Pages 27, 28
Clarence D., Page 28
Dallas, Page 29
Edgar N., Page 28
Effie M., Page 28
Elliott, Page 29
Emmons F., Page 28
Emmons K., Page 28
Ethel G., Page 21
Dr. Eugene C., Page 28
Everts McQ., Page 21
Fred S., Page 28
Gertrude C., Page 28
Harriet E., Page 19
WYLIE
Hattie M., Page 21
Izetta, Page 19
John, Page 23
Lestina, Page 20
Nancy J., Page 20
Parker R., Page 28
Robert, Pages 19, 28
Robert J., Page 28
Russell P., Page 28
Ruth P., Page 28
Sarah E., Page 24
Thomas B., Pages 19, 20
WYMAN
David B., Page 37
Nancy J., Page 107
YOUNG
Gideon, Page 87
Hannah, Pages 13, 37
Lydia, Page 37
Martha, Page 37
Mary, Pages 37, 90
Mary M., Page 36
Peggy, Page 93
Rebecca, Pages 37, 61
Samuel, Page 37
Sidney, Page 87
ZASTRE, Andrew, Page 88